ANTARCTICA

Look for these and other books in the
Lucent Endangered Animals and Habitats series:

The Amazon Rain Forest
The Bald Eagle
The Bear
Bighorn Sheep
Birds of Prey
The Cheetah
Chimpanzees
The Condor
Coral Reefs
The Crocodile
Dolphins and Propoises
The Elephant
Frogs and Toads
The Galapagos Islands
The Giant Panda

The Jaguar
The Koala
The Leopard
The Manatee
The Oceans
The Orangutan
The Rhinoceros
Seals and Sea Lions
The Shark
Snakes
The Tiger
Turtles and Tortoises
The Wetlands
The Whale
The Wolf

Other related titles in the Lucent Overview series:

Acid Rain
Endangered Species
Energy Alternatives
Garbage
The Greenhouse Effect
Hazardous Waste
Ocean Pollution
Oil Spills
Ozone
Pesticides
Population
Rainforests
Recycling
Saving the American Wilderness
Vanishing Wetlands
Zoos

ANTARCTICA

BY DENNIS ROBERSON

Endangered
Animals &
Habitats

LUCENT
BOOKS ®

THOMSON
━━━━✦━━━━ ™
GALE

San Diego • Detroit • New York • San Francisco • Cleveland • New Haven, Conn. • Waterville, Maine • London • Munich

LIBRARY OF CONGRESS CATALOGING-IN-PUBLICATION DATA

Roberson, Dennis.
    Antarctica / by Dennis Roberson.
       p. cm. — (Endangered animals and habitats)
Includes bibliographical references (p.).
Summary: Examines the hostile environment, flora and fauna, minerals, humans,
and ecological efforts to protect the ice continent of Antarctica.
    ISBN 1-56006-727-6 (hardback : alk. paper)
    1. Natural history—Antarctica—Juvenile literature. [1. Antarctica. 2. Endangered
ecosystems. 3. Ecology—Antarctica.] I. Title. II. Endangered animals & habitats.
    QH84.2 .R63 2004
    577.5'86'09989—dc21

                      2002011053

Contents

Introduction

FOR COUNTLESS CENTURIES, while the human race evolved, advanced, and populated the planet, Antarctica's natural and scientific treasures lay hidden and unknown at the bottom of the world. Remote from civilization, Antarctica was engulfed by a dangerous ocean and thousands of miles of ice. However, with its wealth of untold secrets, the frozen continent was destined to eventually become one of the Earth's last great frontiers.

No human ventured close to this frigid, isolated continent until Captain James Cook sailed south of the Antarctic Circle in 1773. Cook did not see the antarctic land mass, however; he saw only the impenetrable fortress of pack ice that surrounded it. But the famous explorer saw enough to conclude that, if someone were to find land beyond the ice, "the world will derive no benefit from it."[1]

Time would soon prove Cook's prediction wrong, and it now seems certain that Antarctica's vast secrets will enrich our knowledge of the world, perhaps even the universe, for many decades.

Explorers

Explorers first reached Antarctica in 1820. They and those who followed told tales about a vicious, unforgiving land of relentless blizzards, deadly glaciers, and bitter cold. Yet they went back, again and again.

In addition to attracting explorers, Antarctica's ocean, coast, and surrounding islands drew hunters and fishermen in search of seals and whales. This hunting drove some

species to the edge of extinction by the end of the 1800s. By then, the challenge of being the first to reach the South Pole beckoned the world's greatest adventurers in a race that fascinated people around the world. The race to the Pole in the early 1900s spawned some of mankind's most heroic and unforgettable tales of adventure, perseverance, survival, and death.

King penguins are just one of the many species that thrive in the frigid environs of Antarctica.

Once explorers reached the South Pole, the quests in Antarctica turned to scientific discovery. Today, the world's focus on the region remains primarily on scientific research, conducted by countries all over the world. Dozens of bases and research stations, some resembling small towns, operate all year long. Researchers study not only the limited (but hardy) animals, plant life, and surrounding marine life, but also the continent's atmosphere and legendary cold climate. They extract from its land and ice not only secrets about the history of the planet and universe, but also clues about Earth's future. Scientists even try to determine what all this research activity is doing to

Antarctica's environment, as well as the effects on humans of long exposure to extreme cold and darkness.

The continent's vast store of ice holds many secrets. Throughout all levels of the massive ice sheet and its glaciers lie clues to the Earth's past, including its former climate and geography. The snowfall of millions of years remains unmelted, containing frozen time capsules of chemicals and gases from past atmospheres. By drilling into the glaciers, scientists can read the history of the Earth's atmosphere and climate, as well as its air pollution. They can tell the specific age of sections of ice and analyze the air bubbles contained within. These tell how the Earth's air evolved and when dramatic temperature changes occurred. They even tell when and where volcanic eruptions took place.

The history and life of Antarctica itself—its glaciers, frozen lakes, rocks, lichens, weather, and wildlife—are unique. Petrified wood, animal bones, and leaf fossils can be found there, telling the story of an ancient, warmer land of many large, vibrant life forms. More than ten thousand meteorites have been recovered from the ice. These space rocks tell much about the history of the solar system. It is possible that Antarctica contains clues to the origins of the universe itself.

Antarctica is an exceptional place for the study of Earth's weather patterns. The cold southern sea water, fed by Antarctica's huge glaciers, affects weather all over the planet. The weather is ultimately controlled by the oceans, and significant changes in Antarctica could have worldwide impact. Scientists also want to use Antarctica to practice exploration planned for Jupiter's

Standing like a frozen time capsule, this majestic iceberg holds the secrets of millions of years of geology.

frozen moons. The continent's scientific potential seems endless, and Antarctica surely holds the answers to questions yet unasked.

David Walton of the British Antarctic Survey explains, "The special environmental characteristics of the continent make it possible to carry out scientific investigations and experiments which are not possible anywhere else in the world."[2] The isolation of small groups of people for long periods of time at remote research stations provides ideal conditions in which psychologists can study group dynamics and personalities. Also, long, controlled isolation lets scientists meticulously study how bacteria travel from one person to another. Unique atmospheric conditions make Antarctica most suitable for studying the Earth's magnetic field and the universe's distant stars. And today, Antarctica is well known as a flashpoint for studies of the earth's ozone and global warming.

Caretakers

Antarctica's unique status as the Earth's only continent with no indigenous people, no government, and thus no protection had placed its future in the balance by the mid-1900s. Human activity had gone unregulated as countries laid huge territorial claims to parts of the continent. Mankind rose to this first challenge by recognizing the political and environmental threats to the region and creating the international Antarctic Treaty, signed by twelve nations in 1959 and enacted in 1961. Many more nations have since signed the treaty so that they, also, could conduct research there.

Governing most of this activity under the Antarctic Treaty are "protocols"—established rules for human behavior on the continent—that are designed to preserve Antarctica's status as a unique world laboratory belonging to all mankind. Projects are limited to peaceful purposes, and all information and research must be shared freely among scientists and nations.

Stringent guidelines for antarctic work and research are intended to protect the fragile environment, but they can be difficult to monitor or enforce. Sometimes regulations are ignored. Bases are abandoned in disarray. Raw sewage is dumped in the ocean. Industrial waste litters the landscape, destroying plant life, as well as bird and animal breeding grounds.

In the last thirty years, significant interest in Antarctica's underground mineral resources has emerged, and in the last ten years tourism has begun to exert pressure on the few crowded, accessible areas during the short summer season. Both of these issues will require additional attention in the future.

An ever increasing human presence on the continent produces inevitable stress on Antarctica's fragile environment. Habitat that is disturbed or contaminated cannot rebound quickly. As technology makes Antarctica more and more accessible, this stress will only increase. A serious push for mineral exploration was halted in 1991 with a new protocol, but its effect is tenuous. Interest in minerals, research, and tourism is now at an all-time high.

Pollutants, like these abandoned and decaying oil drums, threaten the delicate ecological environment of Antarctica.

How mankind manages Antarctica in the twenty-first century may predict how well humans will do with other parts of the world, if not the entire planet or even outer space. This is the challenge that faces a large international cooperative of governments, scientific organizations, watchdog groups, and determined individuals. Although they have declared that Antarctica belongs to everyone, sometimes there are competing interests or differing ideas of how to protect it. As it now stands, what Antarctica's future holds remains in doubt.

1

The Great
Frozen Continent

At the bottom of our planet, in a location incomparably remote and brutally inhospitable, Antarctica is unique among Earth's continents. Towering ice cliffs dwarf everything in sight. Thousands of breeding penguins huddle together for warmth on rocks and ice. Icebergs the size of large cities, or even small countries, float treacherously offshore. Distinct sounds accompany these sights—howling hurricane-force winds, cracking and popping ice, barking seals, and the gigantic, explosive splashes of glaciers calving into the sea. It is the most stark and frigid land on Earth.

At 5.4 million square miles, Antarctica is twice the size of Australia and 50 percent larger than the United States. Yet 99 percent of it cannot be seen. It is buried under a smothering blanket of ice that is an average eight thousand feet thick. In other words, in most places a person would have to dig down through at least one mile of ice to reach land. Mountain ranges are buried beneath. Various exposed mountain peaks, rocky coastlines and islands, and the ice-free "Dry Valleys" of Victoria Land—a coastal region near the Ross Sea—comprise the 1 percent of antarctic land that is visible.

The tremendous weight of the ice actually affects the shape of the planet, flattening it at the South Pole. Ice is also what makes Antarctica the lowest and highest continent on Earth. The average height of the ice sheet makes the continent the tallest overall, while the ice depresses most of the land mass below sea level. Its lowest point, the Bentley Subglacial Trench, sits 8,325 feet *below* sea level. If the ice sheet were removed, most of the continent would rise, or rebound, above sea level.

The antarctic continent has two distinct sections. East Antarctica is the larger plateau section, about 4 million square miles in size, containing the most ice and the South Pole. Just off the coast of East Antarctica rumbles the world's southernmost volcano. Mount Erebus, rising 12,448 feet, features a crater containing a perpetual lava lake—one of only three in the world. Not far away, evidence indicates that a volcano is currently erupting *underneath* the ice sheet, melting surrounding ice from below.

The Transantarctic Mountains separate this giant plateau from smaller West Antarctica, which constitutes only about 25 percent of the continent. This includes the Antarctic Peninsula, the northernmost land of the continent and one of its busiest wildlife and research areas. Vinson Massif,

Mostly covered by sheets of ice, Antarctica's towering mountain ranges are visible in the Dry Valleys of the Ross Sea.

Mount Erebus on Ross Island in East Antarctica contains a perpetual lava lake.

the highest point in Antarctica at 16,067 feet, dominates the coast where the long, curving peninsula joins the main continent.

Pinching the continent at the junction of these two main sections are the Weddell Sea on the Atlantic side and the Ross Sea on the Pacific side. Both are named after early antarctic explorers.

Also contributing to the ecosystem are the antarctic and subantarctic islands. Approximately two dozen islands or island groups dot the ocean around the continent. They are the world's most remote islands, and many are volcanic in origin. Those closest to land, with weather dominated by the continent and/or sea ice, are considered coastal and maritime antarctic islands; those farthest north, with weather defined by the surrounding ocean conditions, are known as subantarctic. With more exposed land and a relatively milder climate, many of the islands provide critical breeding grounds for wildlife.

The climate

Antarctica is referred to as the driest, coldest, and windiest continent on Earth. Furthermore, it is surrounded by the world's stormiest seas. The high central plateau is a brutally cold desert, averaging less than two inches of precipitation per year. Coastal areas receive two to four inches of precipitation annually. This lack of rain or snowfall provides a true paradox of nature: Antarctica's huge ice cap contains three-fourths of the world's fresh water, yet it receives less precipitation today than the Sahara Desert.

The world's lowest recorded temperature ever, −129 degrees Fahrenheit, was recorded on the high ice plateau in 1983. The area's annual mean temperature is between −58 and −76 degrees Fahrenheit. The annual mean temperature at the coast ranges from −4 to +14 degrees Fahrenheit. However, summer temperatures (December–February) at the northern tip of the Antarctic Peninsula have reached

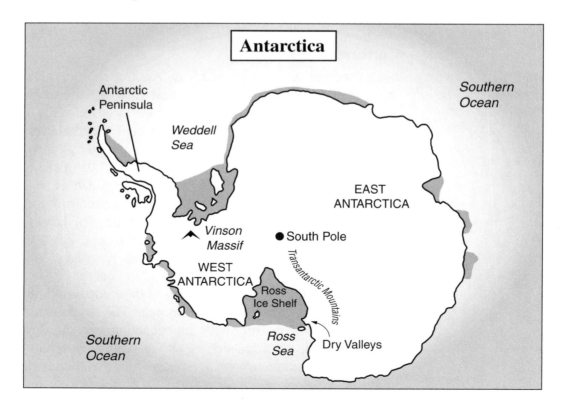

52 degrees Fahrenheit. These warmer temperatures, which also characterize the islands, bring additional precipitation and thus support more plant life than temperatures in the rest of the continent.

Though Antarctica's coastal areas experience higher average temperatures, they suffer relentless gales that can blow fifty miles per hour or more for weeks. Gusts can reach nearly two hundred miles per hour. These turbulent winds are caused by dense, cold air rushing down from the high polar plateau. Known as katabatic winds, they sweep up loose snow to create blinding, blizzardlike conditions, even when the sky above is clear. Experiencing these conditions firsthand inspired early explorer Douglas Mawson to write a book titled *The Home of the Blizzard.*

Antarctica's winters feature months of constant darkness, followed by a summer of continuous sunlight. The dark winter sky provides perfect viewing for the aurora australis, or "southern lights," a magically eerie light display caused by interaction of the sun's energy with the Earth's magnetic field.

Continent of ice

The weight and compression of Antarctica's vast ice sheet create tremendous glaciers that flow off the main continental plateau toward the ocean on all sides. This 7 million cubic miles of ice is the compacted accumulation of one hundred thousand years of snow. The outer glaciers are so big that, upon reaching the coast, not all of them break up. Their tongues stretch out onto the ocean as permanent floating "ice shelves." More than a dozen ring the continent, covering 30 percent of its coastline. The largest is the Ross Ice Shelf, which is as big as France. It is 3,000 feet thick at the coast and 650 feet high where its edge lies in the open ocean.

Icebergs break off of these shelves at their edges and litter the Southern Ocean by the thousands. The largest ones remain for years, drifting with the ocean currents circling Antarctica. One recorded iceberg was as large as Belgium.

Not all of Antarctica's ice emanates from the continent, however. Winter sea ice forms directly on the ocean sur-

face in extreme winter temperatures. Though sea ice exists year-round, in winter it surrounds the entire continent and many of the islands. At that time, its total area is greater than the size of the continent itself. More than three times as much sea ice covers the ocean in winter than in summer.

Antarctica pulsates with this seasonal advance and retreat of sea ice. Sea ice closest to the continental coasts is known as fast ice and is the most calm and stable. Ice that extends well out into the ocean is known as pack ice. It can be extremely unstable—cracking, breaking up, colliding, and moving constantly with the winds and ocean currents. Antarctica's sea ice is so extensive that it affects heat exchange between ocean and atmosphere and thus has an impact on global weather patterns as well as marine life.

Although the antarctic weather limits survival and diversity, under the ice shelves and sea ice the protected ocean and sea floor teem with life. This provides a bountiful marine food supply for the birds and mammals of Antarctica.

A 650-foot wall of ice shows the seaward edge of the massive Ross Ice Shelf.

Krill

Krill are tiny shrimplike creatures living throughout the Southern Ocean that grow to be one to two inches long. Millions of krill often swim in huge, dense swarms that represent hundreds of tons of food to their predators. Krill consume microscopic algae, or phytoplankton, that thrive in the cold, nutrient-rich waters around Antarctica. Algae float near the surface and cling to the ice, where they are consumed by krill.

"[Krill] are the common currency here," explains antarctic researcher Roger Hewitt. "Everything eats them, from hundred-ton blue whales to seals and penguins, birds and fish, right on down to the tiny zooplankton that feed on krill larvae."[3] For some species, krill is almost the entire diet.

To have so many different animal species dependent on one food source is very unusual. Furthermore, those species that eat mostly fish or squid are indirectly dependent on krill as well. Without abundant krill, the ecosystem of the Southern Ocean and Antarctica would collapse.

Penguins

Perhaps the animal most identified with Antarctica is the penguin. The antarctic coast, its ice, and the surrounding islands provide critical breeding grounds for these warm-blooded, flightless birds. Though some penguins spend as much as 75 percent of their life in the ocean, Antarctica is where the world's southernmost species breed, lay their eggs, raise their young, and protect their young from predators. With suitable breeding grounds scattered, penguins form huge breeding colonies known as rookeries, many containing tens or hundreds of thousands of birds.

Penguins are well suited to their environment. Their outer layer of densely packed feathers provides not only warmth but also waterproofing. A thick layer of blubber underneath adds to their insulation and energy store.

On land, penguins are fairly safe from predators, though seabirds will attack vulnerable chicks. In the sea, penguins are hunted by killer whales and some seals. Four penguin species breed on the antarctic continent, peninsula, and is-

lands—the emperor, Adelie, gentoo, and chinstrap—with other species utilizing only certain antarctic islands.

The emperor penguin is the world's largest, growing more than three feet tall and weighing over sixty pounds. Its "royal" look comes from the gold-accented neck feathers and a matching stripe on the lower beak. Amazingly, it breeds mostly on fast ice during the brutal and dark winter. It is the only antarctic bird to do so, the only one large enough to survive the difficult winter fast.

Emperor courtship and incubation take about three months. The male incubates a single egg on its feet and under its feathers, huddling close with other penguins to conserve heat. This incubation survives average temperatures of minus 4 degrees Fahrenheit and winds gusting to more than one hundred miles per hour. Once the female lays her egg, she disappears into the ocean for two months, gorging herself. Meanwhile the male loses 40 percent of his weight by fasting during the long incubation.

A large colony of penguins huddles together on land. Penguins have become the animal most identified with Antarctica.

The severe conditions mean that emperors cannot afford to expend energy. No one fights over territory. They stand shoulder to shoulder, silent and almost motionless, though rotating positions so no bird stays on the outer edge of the group. In addition to huddling together, the fathers-to-be recover 80 percent of the heat in their breath through a nasal-passage heat-exchange system.

Emperor chicks are born in July, the dead of Antarctica's winter, but need several more months to grow and achieve independence. The end of this critical growth period must occur in spring when pack ice is breaking up, making the sea and food most accessible.

This emperor penguin chick will have to struggle against the harsh Antarctic environment to reach maturity.

Mothers return when the eggs hatch in July to relieve the fathers, who then make a dark and deadly trek across the wide sea ice to find the ocean and replenish themselves. The parents share feeding duty while the chicks huddle together. If the ice has not begun breaking up sufficiently at this time, the parents must travel farther to the sea, causing many chicks to die of starvation. Only 40 percent of emperor chicks survive to maturity.

Early antarctic explorer Apsley Cherry-Garrard observes, "All in all I do not believe anybody on earth has a worse time than the Emperor Penguin."[4]

The Adelie penguin has stark, simple black-and-white coloring. This small species, weighing about eleven pounds and twenty-seven inches tall, is probably the most widely distributed and most-studied bird of Antarctica. Adelies lay two eggs on pebble nests in rookeries on the coast of Antarctica or its islands. The parents share both incubation and feeding of the chicks. Adelies are known for remarkable "homing" capabilities and are believed to navigate by the sun.

Other penguins of the antarctic and subantarctic islands are the macaroni, king, and rockhopper. The macaroni penguins are the most abundant species of the entire region, numbering more than 23 million, and they breed as far south as the South Shetland Islands just off the Antarctic Peninsula.

Flying seabirds

Numerous other magnificent birds, especially those of the albatross and petrel families, depend on Antarctica for nesting habitat. In some cases they even compete with penguins and seals for precious breeding space. While most prefer the antarctic islands, nineteen species of seabirds breed on the continent. These ocean-ranging seabirds feed mostly on squid and fish, and they stay warm by using their thick down feathers to trap an insulating layer of air next to their body. They number more than 100 million, and the largest of them is the giant wandering albatross, with an eleven-foot wingspan. The majestic albatross can live up to eighty-five years. Its long life helps offset the high mortality rate of its chicks, which is often as much as 50 percent.

Albatross parents lay one egg in the summer, and it incubates for up to eighty days. The young wandering albatross needs nine months before it can survive on its own. This means that the parents, who mate for life, reproduce only every other year.

After hatching, the wandering albatross chick is fed about every three days. The parents alternate feedings, leaving to forage in the ocean for six days at a time. It takes that long for a parent to consume enough food for itself and the chick. Like penguins, it regurgitates food to its offspring upon returning. Once able to fly, the young

A wandering albatross hovers over Antarctica's Southern Ocean. Albatross have the ability to fly above the ocean for years before setting foot on land.

albatross will soar about the ocean for *years* before ever setting foot on land again.

Very little is known about albatross's activity at sea, where they spend most of their lives. It is believed that they hunt the sea at night, when elusive creatures such as squid rise close to the surface to feed. Legendary fliers, albatross can travel thousands of miles in a single trip. They navigate the strong winds and storms of the Southern Ocean almost effortlessly.

"There is a sense in which the Wandering Albatross knew, long before we men, that the earth was a globe," remarks naturalist Louis J. Halle, "for in their navigation they return to their nesting sites by continuing in the direction of their departure, making a circuit of the earth."[5]

Several species of petrel populate the antarctic environment. They usually burrow into the soil of islands, tucked among tussock grasses, or nest in lava cracks, visiting mostly at night and feeding at sea during the day. While most of these birds breed near the coast, the snow and antarctic petrels sometimes nest hundreds of miles inland on the cliffs of exposed antarctic mountain peaks, called nunataks.

Some petrels are scavengers. Giant petrels feed on seal carcasses and can kill penguins or other birds. "Around the nests we've also found seal skin, squid beaks and krill," notes seabird researcher Donna Patterson. "They're doing their job, cleaning up the Southern Ocean."[6]

Other antarctic birds rarely venture far from the coast for feeding. These are the cormorants, gulls, sheathbills, terns, and skuas.

Skuas, known as the ugliest of antarctic birds because of their hooked beaks, prey on penguin eggs and chicks, or other young birds. Outside the breeding season, they patrol the water for krill and fish. Though they typically lay two eggs each year on nests of pebbles, moss, and bones, skuas raise only the first chick that hatches. They are aggressive and often chase other seabirds to force them to drop their prey or regurgitate, then steal the food out of the air before it drops into the sea. The south polar skua is the world's southernmost bird, occasionally appearing at the South Pole.

Seals

The largest mammals to use Antarctica's coast, islands, and ice are seals, who depend on them mainly for breeding grounds. Once the victims of the earliest commercial exploitation of the Antarctic's resources, some of the seven area species were hunted to near extinction. Seals use blubber or fur for insulation, which serves them well in the water as well as out of it. Like penguins, seals appear awkward on land but swim with grace, speed, and skill.

The crabeater seal is the most abundant of all seals, numbering from 30 million to 40 million. The name is misleading, for its diet consists mostly of krill. Unique five-pointed teeth act like a strainer, allowing the seal to hold the krill in its mouth while expelling seawater.

Crabeaters prefer the treacherous pack ice to land, and they are very territorial. Thus not as much is known about

Race for the Pole

Norwegian explorer Roald Amundsen planned to be the first man to reach the North Pole. He had already been the first to navigate the long-sought-after Northwest Passage (the northern shipping route across the top of North America) and the first to spend the winter south of the Antarctic Circle. But American Robert Peary bagged that honor instead, by reaching the North Pole first in 1909. (That same year Irishman Ernest Shackleton came within about one hundred miles of the South Pole but was forced to retreat by a lack of sufficient food supplies.) At that time, Amundsen turned his attention to Antarctica, where the South Pole remained unreached by man. His competition would be famed British explorer Robert Scott, who had failed to reach the South Pole in 1902 and was mounting another expedition.

Amundsen's team set off inland from the antarctic coast on October 19, 1911. Five days later, using a different route, Scott's team began its trek. Amundsen's trip was practically flawless, and he reached the South Pole on December 14, 1911, taking less than sixty days. On January 12, thirty-five days later than Amundsen, Scott reached the South Pole only to find a note in a tent left by his rival. Crushed, Scott and his men began their return but tragically were overtaken by blizzards and starvation, dying just eleven miles from their next food depot.

Norwegian explorer Roald Amundsen was the first to reach the South Pole in 1911.

their behavior, and their exact numbers are difficult to obtain. Born on the ice, pups weigh about forty pounds. Like all nonharem species, crabeater females grow to be as big as, or bigger than, males. This allows them to survive the energy-depleting activity of raising their young alone.

The southern elephant seal is the world's largest seal, with males growing to fifteen feet and weighing four tons. Their name comes from their size and their inflatable, extended noses that resemble the stump of an elephant trunk. When inflated, the nose enhances a resonating bellow that helps to intimidate rival males.

Elephant seals feed mainly on squid, diving more than a mile deep and for up to two hours in search of food. To accomplish this, their heart can slow to as little as one beat per minute. Males haul themselves out on the antarctic island beaches at the end of winter, followed by the much smaller females. The males then fight for the title of "beachmaster," which earns them a harem of up to thirty females. Pups weigh one hundred pounds at birth and, on a diet of rich mother's milk, can weigh four hundred pounds at only three weeks.

Antarctic fur seals are nimble out of water compared with other species. They can turn their hind legs forward underneath their body and, using their fore flippers, walk or even "gallop" on land or ice. Males possess a distinct mane around their neck and shoulders, and small ear flaps adorn both sexes. Their fur coat features two layers that trap air for insulation. This makes up for their species' thin blubber layer. The fur seal diet consists of krill, fish, and squid.

Using mostly sandy island beaches, the males arrive in early spring. The females emerge weeks later at the onset of summer and give birth within two days. The seals repeat six- to nine-day cycles of feeding at sea and returning to feed their young during a four-month suckling period. During this time the vigilant males defend their harems and territory, losing a lot of weight in the process. Their teeth can inflict severe wounds.

Like the crabeater, very little is known about the behavior of the Ross seal. It lives deep in the pack ice and is difficult to observe. When seen, it is almost always either alone or one of a pair. It feeds mainly on fish and squid and is easily identified by its large eyes, short and wide head, and very long rear flippers. The Ross is also the smallest antarctic seal, growing to about seven feet and four hundred pounds.

Conversely, the most-studied antarctic seal is the Weddell seal. It breeds on the stable fast ice near the coast and is easily approached. The females can grow to a length of ten feet and can weigh up to eight hundred pounds when they gather on the ice around breathing holes in the spring to give birth. Weddells can dive very deep and stay under for more than an hour, feeding on fish, squid, and krill. During the dark winter they live underwater, where it is warmer, continually gnawing and scraping away at the ice with their teeth to keep open breathing holes. Though equipped with large eyes to accommodate low-light conditions, the Weddell uses sonar to locate food and find its way back to the breathing holes.

Finally, the leopard seal is the fiercest predator of the group. Named for their spots, leopard seals are built for speed, and they have a wide variety of prey. Though they eat a lot of krill, they also take birds, including penguins, and young crabeater seals. Traveling and hunting alone, their cunning and ferocity are well known. After catching a penguin, leopard seals thrash it about violently before eating it.

Tough plants and microscopic life

While a few marine animals and birds use insulation and mobility to survive in Antarctica, the incredibly cold, relentless wind and long periods of darkness all but prohibit other life on the continent. The scarcity of exposed land also limits whatever life forms could exist. Yet communities of bacteria, algae, fungi, and tiny insects do exist there.

The wingless midge, a fly that can grow up to one-half inch in length, is the *largest* animal in Antarctica to live entirely on land. Another one hundred or so species of microscopic insects include mites, springtails, lice, fleas, and nematodes (worms). Some are barely visible to the naked

eye. They survive temperatures well below freezing with the help of glycerol, a natural antifreeze. This enables their body fluids to remain liquid despite temperatures well below freezing.

Insects that do not scavenge (feed on dead seals and birds) either prey on other insects or eat algae and fungi. These creatures survive almost exclusively on the Antarctic Peninsula and islands, where conditions are less extreme. They are usually found under rocks and around mosses, especially in or near penguin rookeries.

Numerous species of mosses, lichens, algae, and bacteria cling to a harsh life in the bitter cold. They can be found on exposed rock or soil along the coast, high on mountaintops, and in the Dry Valleys of Victoria Land. Bacteria are even found in snow at the South Pole, and some lichen live within a few hundred miles of there. The most remarkable types of these organisms actually live *inside* rocks, especially in the Dry Valleys. Settling into cracks near the rock

Striking an almost playful pose, this leopard seal is among the fiercest predators of the Antarctic.

Where Does Antarctica Stop?

The term *Antarctica* is often used to describe the entire southern portion of the Earth as opposed to just the continent of that name. This is because the land, ice, ocean, and climate are so interdependent. While the Antarctic Treaty defines sixty degrees latitude as the border of its control, this is not a meaningful biological or geographic distinction. Nor is the Antarctic Circle, which simply marks the northernmost point where twenty-four hours of light or darkness can be experienced and does not even entirely contain the antarctic continent. The most accepted scientific boundary is an imaginary, wavy, constantly moving line in the ocean called the Antarctic Convergence. It marks the point where the cold surface waters of the Southern Ocean meet with the warmer waters of the more northern oceans. South of the convergence line, the water temperature immediately drops by about five degrees Fahrenheit. This mixing of waters creates an upwelling of life and nutrients along the convergence line. It also spawns cold, wet, and windy weather. Most of the subantarctic islands lie close to the Antarctic Convergence, which generally falls between fifty and sixty-two degrees south latitude.

surface, they receive just enough sunlight for photosynthesis. However, their growth rate is so slow that some of these organisms could be thousands of years old.

Large types of lichen and moss grow several feet deep on the Antarctic Peninsula and islands. These, too, are hundreds or thousands of years old and are very susceptible to disturbance. They compete for space with penguins and seals and often are trampled to death. Only algae can survive the beating. In dense colonies the animal waste is so thick as to be toxic to plants. Moderate or light waste levels from small colonies, however, can enrich the surrounding plant community, and antarctic plants can quickly colonize abandoned breeding areas.

Lichens are able to absorb water vapor from ice or snow and actually grow best when under a thin layer of snow.

They are actually a combination of a fungus and an alga; the fungus provides water and the alga provides nutrients. This "job-sharing" design makes lichens the most successful and best-adapted plant of Antarctica, withstanding long periods of drought or cold.

Lichens grow almost exclusively on rocks or stones. Snow acts as a layer of insulation during winter, preventing extreme temperature changes. Algae and fungi are found growing on many moss stems, providing food for microscopic insects. The bottoms of some of Antarctica's frozen lakes are carpeted with moss or algae, which have adapted to the low-light conditions.

Several species of snow algae live in patches on the surface ice of Antarctica, giving it a red, pink, yellow, or green tint. Another species of brown algae grows in the sea ice, providing food for krill. "Mother Nature has a remarkable power of producing life everywhere; even the ice is a fruitful soil for her," remarks oceanographer Miles McPhee.[7]

No trees or shrubs could ever survive here, but two flowering plants, antarctic hair grass and antarctic pearlwort, do. They occur in small clumps on the west coast of the Antarctic Peninsula. The maritime and subantarctic islands, farther north, are able to support more plant life. Many contain extensive tussock grass meadows attractive to seabirds and some penguins for nesting.

Antarctica's unforgiving climate and terrain make life possible only for those plants and creatures most highly adapted to such brutal conditions. They also create a frozen landscape and seascape like no others in the world. Antarctica is a true frontier and, despite the increasing human presence, will likely remain so for a very long time.

2

Human Impact on a Fragile Land

ANTARCTICA IS A continent, not a country. There are no towns, no native human population, no culture, no capital city. Nor does Antarctica belong to any country. Undisturbed by humans for thousands of years, Antarctica's relatively recent discovery has drawn people to the bottom of the Earth in ever increasing numbers. Impacts on the ecosystem have been inflicted by hunters and fishermen, researchers and scientists, and now tourists.

Hunters and fishermen

Antarctica's earliest explorers were so few in numbers, and their tools so crude, that they had little impact on the environment other than killing birds and seals for food. Their reports back to civilization, however, brought commercial sealers in droves. Thus it was Antarctica's wildlife that felt the first brutal blow from humans.

Throughout the 1800s, fur seals were slaughtered to near extinction for their dense coats. Then hunters killed elephant seals for the oil in their blubber. Finally, with so few seals left, commercial sealing all but disappeared by the early 1900s. Left in its wake were 3 million dead fur seals. (About this time, whales in the Southern Ocean became the hunters' targets, meeting the same deadly fate during the twentieth century.)

Sealing and whaling are either outlawed or severely restricted today, and the seal populations have rebounded over the last one hundred years to about where they were before. The devastated whale populations never did, though, with some species estimated to be at only 1 to 3 percent of their original levels. Their destruction is believed to have had another environmental effect. The huge amount of krill, squid, and fish that these mammals once consumed became available to other animal species. Though scientists do not know exact population numbers from the 1800s and early 1900s, it is generally believed that non-hunted seal species, as well as penguins and other seabirds, grew in numbers as the ocean's available food supply increased.

In the late twentieth century, commercial fishing operations moved into the Southern Ocean in search of an unexploited resource. Part of what drove fishermen this far south was the depletion of fish stocks throughout the

 Easy Targets

During the 1800s hunters slaughtered fur seals annually by the hundreds of thousands. They stopped—around 1900—only when there were not enough seals left with which to bother. One veteran sealer testified to the U.S. Congress in 1892, "We killed everything, old and young, that we could get in gunshot of, excepting the black pups, whose skins were unmarketable, and most of all these died of starvation, having no means of sustenance, or else were killed by a sort of buzzard, when the mother seals, having been destroyed, were unable to protect them longer. . . . As it is, however, seals in the Antarctic regions are practically extinct, and I have given up the business as unprofitable." Another sealer testified, "During the latter part of a season the seals become very wild, and we used to shoot them in the water from boats. When we shoot them in the water, we lose certainly three out of five we kill by sinking, and we also wounded a great many more. Shooting seals in the water is the most destructive method of taking them as compared with the number of skins we have to show for our work."

rest of the world from decades of overfishing in other oceans.

The commercial fishing industry has a significant impact on antarctic wildlife. Fishing operations deplete marine food resources and kill many birds in the process. The current catch volumes of toothfish, squid, and krill are growing, and any overharvesting of the primary animal food sources in Antarctica could quickly destroy the entire ecosystem. The Antarctic Treaty nations' 1978 Convention on the Conservation of Antarctic Marine Living Resources (CCAMLR) sought to rein in catch levels, document harvesting, and manage the marine ecosystem. In practice, however, countries can veto or ignore regulations, and illegal fishing is rampant. One of the most popular targets at this time is the toothfish, often called sea bass in stores and restaurants. It is estimated that at least 40 to 50 percent of the annual toothfish catch is illegal.

The Southern Ocean's seabirds hunt the waters for food and are lured by commercial fishing fleets that drop bait lines and hooks. The birds, including rare and threatened petrels and albatross, dive for the fish food and are killed or injured in droves by the sinking hooks.

"We've found hooks and lines around the nests, as well as hooks engorged in the birds' throats," remarked researcher Donna Patterson.[8] Bird census studies show that the population of various albatross, as well as the giant petrel, are crashing as a result. Strict regulations under the Antarctic Treaty attempt to balance the amount of legal fishing with the needs and protection of wildlife. Nonetheless, estimates indicate that the fishing fleets kill as many as one hundred thousand antarctic birds annually. Many of these operations are illegal under the Antarctic Treaty, but so far attempts to stop them have failed.

Ten species of Southern Ocean seabirds have been captured on such fishing gear, commonly albatross and petrels, and the impact on their populations can be severe. The wandering albatross is now classified as a globally threatened species because of drops in numerous monitored colonies for years.

Scientists

After the South Pole was reached for the first time in 1911, the focus on Antarctica turned to science. Countries all over the world sent expeditions and built research bases from which their scientists could work. This activity grew continuously over the first half of the century, with a dozen nations seeking to learn from the unique environment.

Antarctica beckoned scientists from all disciplines, and they came to study the weather, wildlife, plant life, ice and glaciers, geography, minerals, and much more. Yet despite the immense size of the icy continent, there were relatively few practical locations for building bases. The research bases were crowded into the 1 percent of area that stayed ice-free—the same 1 percent that was home to most of Antarctica's wildlife. Even worse, no rules or laws governed the area. This led to many negative effects on the antarctic ecosystem. The establishment and growth of research bases produced an equivalent creation of trash dumps and sewage. What was not piled up on land or incinerated in open pits was dumped into the ocean.

"When I first began work in the Antarctic in 1967, recycling was not even considered in many research stations and dumping waste in remote areas of the Antarctic was a common practice," confirms researcher David Walton of the British Antarctic Survey. "Unfortunately, in the low temperatures characteristic of the Antarctic, there is virtually no bacterial decay, so the wastes associated with scientific stations and with this laissez-faire attitude of earlier days are still with us."[9]

Building and operating bases not only produced lots of garbage, but also emitted heat, noise, dust, and gases. All over Antarctica's coastal areas, toxic pollutants leached into the fragile soil; incinerated waste released toxic gases into the air; and discarded machinery piled up to become an eyesore. Sewage and some garbage floated out to sea on sea ice or was dumped straight onto the ocean floor, and other trash just lay out in open heaps or "tips," threatening scavenging birds that ate from them. (Tips are open waste dumps that contain any trash or discarded equipment not

Piles of rubbish at Mawson Base are the result of many years of careless handling of waste by researchers who once inhabited the antarctic station.

burned or dumped in the ocean.) Ships servicing these bases occasionally leaked or spilled oil, which washed ashore. Onshore, storage tanks, machinery, and vehicles repeatedly spilled fluid.

In 1972 a small U.S. nuclear reactor in Antarctica was shut down after ten years of problems. Built on the flank of volcanic Mount Erebus, its cleanup required the removal of thousands of cubic yards of contaminated soil and rocks. It took another six years before the site was deemed safe for general human access.

Even those people and bases trying to minimize impact can only do so much. The United States' McMurdo Station on Ross Island off the antarctic coast recorded 323 fuel spills from 1991 to 1998 that poured thousands of gallons of fuel onto the surrounding environment. These were due mostly to "leaks from rubber bladders, seals and fittings,"[10] used on various types of machinery and equipment. The diesel-fueled heavy machinery often used to build and operate such bases produces greater pollution in Antarctica's extreme cold temperatures than in milder climates because the engines work less efficiently in such conditions.

Much of the environmental focus in Antarctica has centered on cleaning up the trash dumps and toxic wastes that have built up over the last fifty years. Australian scientists "estimate the volume of abandoned, unconfined tip materials in Antarctica is somewhere between 1 and 10 million cubic meters, and that the volume of petroleum-contaminated sediment is similar."[11] Sometimes analysis shows that cleaning up certain sites would cause more environmental damage than merely leaving them alone. In these cases, either getting to the site with the necessary equipment would destroy the surrounding environment or the handling and moving of the waste would release the pollutants into a larger area than is currently exposed.

Even if humans could operate waste-free in Antarctica, its remoteness would still not completely protect it from man-made pollution. Researchers at Terra Nova Bay station in the Ross Sea have proved that "minute particles of lead from gasoline combustion are blown to Antarctica as soon as one month after they have left exhaust pipes in South America, Australia and New Zealand," notes Jeff Rubin in *Lonely Planet Antarctica*.[12] Indeed, minute traces of man-made chemicals used in other parts of the world are now being detected in the snow that falls over the region. They are becoming concentrated in the bodies of local wildlife such as seals and penguins.

In addition to creating pollution and waste, research bases have altered the plants and soil forever. According to researcher Kaye Everett:

> "Any activity which covers or removes or in other ways disturbs all or any part of the soil profile, such as landscape reshaping, excavation and road-building, destroys the soil—a product of climate, vegetation and site variables which have been interacting for periods of time measurable in decades to millennia and in the case of the Dry Valleys, millions of years. Restoration of an area, in the sense of restoring the natural contour or filling and the like does not and cannot restore the soil or the soil organisms."[13]

Nuclear Power

Although the Antarctic Treaty bans nuclear explosions and nuclear waste dumping, it does not forbid the use of nuclear power. In 1961–1962, the U.S. Navy installed an experimental, water-pressurized nuclear reactor near its McMurdo base in an attempt to find a more economical way of providing heat and power. The reactor was located near Mount Erebus, an active volcano, and the following ten years of operation told a disappointing story of expensive shutdowns, fire damage, and radiation leaks. In 1972 a temporary shutdown caused by a coolant water leak coincided with a Navy cost-effectiveness study. The report concluded that it would be too expensive to upgrade the plant, so it was closed and torn down over the course of three years, at a cost of $1 million.

The reactor and 101 large drums of radioactive earth were shipped back to the United States for burial. Later, another 14,500 cubic yards of soil and rock were also shipped to the United States. Six more years of cleanup finally led to the site being declared decontaminated to levels as low as reasonably achievable, and the area became available for unrestricted use in 1979.

Additionally, people working on land could not help but trample much of the surroundings. The cold antarctic environment is so harsh that just a misplaced human footprint can have a lasting negative impact.

"The slow growth of Antarctic mosses means that the mark of a footprint remains in a mossbank for some considerable time," states I. Iverson of the British Antarctic Survey. "The break in the surface at the edge of the footprint allows the wind to grip the surface and tear the moss bank apart, causing erosion at a rate far faster than the rate at which moss can grow."[14]

Indeed, a moss bed footprint can still be seen in Antarctica more than ten years after it was made. "Some moss beds on the Antarctic Peninsula have taken three to four hundred years to grow; a single human footprint can cause tremendous damage and remain there as a permanent record," emphasizes William Fraser of Montana State University.[15]

Trampling is but one threat to plant life. Scarce, fragile, and dependent on water, the vegetation is vulnerable to any changes in snow melting patterns or changes in drainage. Antarctic lichens have even been killed by coal ash deposited from a nearby station.

Man-made pollution and trampling caused by research bases are accompanied by a serious disturbance of wildlife habitat. In the late 1950s, a joint U.S.–New Zealand station at Hallett on the Ross Sea coast had been set in the middle of a penguin rookery, displacing six thousand birds. A barricade of fuel drums met those birds that tried to return to their annual nesting grounds. Although this base closed in 1973, twenty years later cleanup teams discovered a twenty-thousand-gallon fuel tank and several smaller tanks still containing fuel. Though two years were spent trying to clean

The image of penguins mingling with a mound of garbage shows the direct impact pollution has on Antarctica's fragile environment.

it up in the 1990s, in 2001 an environmental survey team still found melt pools and Adelie penguin chicks contaminated with oil. (Melt pools are localized ponds of melted snow or ice.)

France's 1983 attempt to blast out an airstrip near its station at Terre Adelie caused great controversy. Eight bird species had used the area for breeding. The site, rich in antarctic wildlife and plants, became a killing field of explosions. Adelie penguins and an estimated fifteen hundred eggs were destroyed in the construction process. After the base's establishment, the neighboring emperor penguin colony plummeted to nearly half its former size. The new airstrip cut off the best access to this colony and destroyed nesting areas for thousands of other birds. Researchers discovered that just one person standing within twenty-five yards of the penguins' pathway to the sea caused the birds to significantly alter their favored route—even hours after the person had left.

Seals, too, showed they were sensitive to human presence. "It appears that placement . . . of temporary living quarters near a seal colony can affect the distribution of seals at the colony," reported the National Science Foundation. "In particular, seals tend to move away from such structures as the season progresses."[16]

Helicopters cause an even greater disruption to wildlife activity. At the very least, such repeated human disturbances cause animals to needlessly expend precious energy.

"The Antarctic ecosystem is an ecosystem under stress, limited by a shortage of solar energy and heat," note Antarctica researchers Creina Bond and Roy Siegfried. "Those huge populations of Antarctic birds and mammals are not signs of great fertility—they are signs of a system that lacks energy, lacks complexity, lacks diversity. Such a system is vulnerable to interference."[17]

The historic Antarctic Treaty signed in 1959 set aside all territorial claims and dedicated human activity in the region to the free pursuit and exchange of science. This truly was, and is, a breakthrough for international cooperation not seen anywhere else on Earth. But as significant and widely

Base Building

There are more than fifty research bases in Antarctica, and building them is difficult. Those built on islands or rocky coastlines are conventional in design and, where possible, are anchored to a rock platform. Still, these locations encounter problems with accessibility and isolation in the harsh Southern Ocean. Bases built on the ice, or ice shelves, of the antarctic continent pose unique problems. The ice is always moving and often unstable, making a solid foundation impossible. Buildings also give off heat, melting the ice directly beneath them, and then sink—some as much as thirty feet before being replaced.

Strong winds build huge snowdrifts in and around buildings and equipment—snowdrifts that never melt. The weight of the accumulating ice and snow can eventually collapse the building. The United States' Byrd station was covered completely within five years of being built.

Radical designs have appeared to fight these problems. Australia built a base on a raised platform facing the wind, so that snow blew underneath it. A new Byrd station was built in a large man-made trench cut out of the ice. The building contained an arched steel roof to further protect it from wind and snow. South Africa put portable buildings inside a steel tunnel, better able to withstand the weight of the ice and snow.

The Amundsen–Scott base at the South Pole was covered by a huge geodesic dome in the 1970s. The original base had not only sunk thirty-three feet into the ice, but also moved more than 1,100 yards away from the South Pole. The United States began completely rebuilding that base for the third time in 2001.

A typical modern base contains several building sections—living quarters, laboratories, radio station, weather station, generator or other power source, and storage. These buildings might be connected by corridors, sometimes underground. Also, most bases have an emergency shelter some distance away in case of a bad fire, a constant worry in the dry antarctic air.

heralded as this document was, it served merely as a political and scientific framework and failed to address serious issues that now confront all of the participating parties.

One of those issues is humans' direct impact on the antarctic environment and wildlife with their waste—trash, sewage, scrap metal, old machinery, chemicals, and so on. The Scientific Committee on Antarctic Research (SCAR) recognized the growing problem and in 1985 issued a report demanding attention to the issue of pollution and environmental damage. (SCAR is a committee of the International Council of Science, created during the formation of the original Antarctic Treaty to promote and coordinate scientific research in Antarctica.)

The SCAR report on this growing human interference claims "the majority of existing research stations were established in their current localities because these were the most convenient places for either logistical or scientific reasons, and without thought for environmental effects."[18] The report singles out Australia's Casey station as an especially dangerous ecological hazard because there was no separation of toxic materials from other noncombustible wastes. Dead skuas were found around the trash, and the birds had themselves spread much of the toxic garbage outside of the pit area.

This effort drew attention to the pollution problem, but the situation was already out of control. Furthermore, the guidelines called for were self-policing, meaning each country was still responsible for its own activities.

"Without doubt, the worst affected place on Antarctica has to be the Fildes Peninsula," observed Susan Sabella of the environmental group Greenpeace in the late 1990s. "There are bases built on moss beds, fuel and chemical drums spilling over onto plant life, there's an airstrip, a lake being used as a landfill—it's appalling. Large moss beds of the kind that were found at Fildes are incredibly rare in Antarctica; this was a special place, but now it's a mess."[19]

In 1991 Antarctic Treaty nations tried to finish what SCAR had started, issuing the Protocol on Environmental Protection to the Antarctic Treaty. This document laid out stringent guidelines for human activity on or near the frozen continent, all geared toward protecting the environment, plants, and wildlife. But it took seven years for all of the participating nations to ratify it, thus postponing its legal effect until 1998. While some nations began implementing the rules after 1991, others did not. Greenpeace site surveys in 1993 and 1995 showed blatant garbage and dumping abuses continuing, with the staff at one location expressing complete ignorance of the protocol's existence.

Still, as more environmentally sensitive practices took hold at the turn of the century, the extent of human activity continued unabated. Early research bases had been relatively small and efficient—huts took up minimal space. Today, some bases resemble small towns. McMurdo station is even called "MacTown" by the locals. With 1,100 residents during the summer, it includes a busy airport, ATMs, and a shuttle bus. The United States is also in the process of completely rebuilding its Amundsen–Scott South Pole station. It will include more than sixty structures.

A view of the sprawling McMurdo station from Observation Hill. Research bases have become quite extensive in recent years.

Tourists

The most stress from human presence occurs in Antarctica each spring and summer, when more scientists and support staff arrive for research. The majority of scientists, several thousand in the summer and about one thousand in the winter, live and work on the continent or ice shelves twenty-four hours per day. Now an increase in tourists adds to these numbers. Tourists greatly outnumber the scientists, but they spend dramatically less time on land. Most cruise from spot to spot in ships, going ashore only a few hours at a time.

Still, in many of the same areas where wildlife and researchers struggle to share space, now come tourists by the thousands. "Whereas once it was the last great wilderness, now Antarctica is being marketed as just the newest, most exotic travel location," observes Alan Hemmings, senior adviser to the Antarctic and Southern Ocean Coalition (ASOC).[20]

Tourists take a boat ride around Cuerva Cove on the Antarctic Peninsula. Some believe the presence of tourists is upsetting the ecological balance in Antarctica.

Most antarctic tourists arrive by ship from November through February—the spring/summer season. The vessels may carry anywhere from three dozen to hundreds of people, all seeking a view of the region's unique scenery and fascinating wildlife. This is the time when the winter sea ice retreats and Antarctica's animals are most active and visible.

In 1996–1997 thirteen ships carried more than 7,000 people to Antarctica. The following two seasons, about 10,000 tourists made the voyage. Then in 1999–2000, the number of tourists surpassed the 14,000 mark. The following season, just over 12,000 tourists visited Antarctica. A small number of visitors venture over the South Pole by air on flight tours, and some adventure tourists come with mountain-climbing, sea-kayaking, and ski-trekking itineraries.

The overwhelming majority of people visit the Antarctic Peninsula and subantarctic islands. This is due to a combination of several factors—milder climate, greater concentration of wildlife activity, and more easily navigable waters—compared with the antarctic areas further south.

However, this recent tourism explosion coincided with the dramatic turn toward environmental concern in Antarctica. Tour operators formed an alliance, the International Association of Antarctic Tour Operators (IAATO), and set up guidelines for shepherding their clients around the popular antarctic sites. Their rules establish that visitors should not approach wildlife closely, tread on plant life, or litter. Generally, operators coordinate their landings so that no two groups visit the same place at the same time, and guides keep a close watch on tourists while on land.

However, just like other Antarctic Treaty guidelines, such rules are easier to write than to enforce. Each tour operator is entrusted with the responsibility to educate the tourists and conduct each trip properly. After all, it is in the operators' best interests for tourism not to have a negative impact on Antarctica.

As tourism escalated in the late 1990s, Darrel Schoeling of the IAATO agreed, stating that part of the organization's mission is "creating ambassadors to the last continent."[21]

A tourist gets up close to a group of chinstrap penguins. This type of activity is discouraged by organizations that oversee antarctic tourist expeditions.

Some tourist expeditions are even sponsored by scientific organizations, such as the Smithsonian Institution or the World Wildlife Fund. Some environmental groups, however, oppose tourism in Antarctica entirely.

Both tourism expert Thomas Bauer and wildlife researcher William Fraser feel that many media accounts accusing tourism of serious negative impacts on the environment are exaggerated or erroneous. One antarctic researcher and tourist guide remarks that "as a group, the passengers on the tourist ships that I have been associated with have had a far greater appreciation, awareness and understanding of the practical needs for protecting and conserving Antarctic wildlife and environment" than many researchers or ship crews.[22]

A tourist's letter to the *New York Times*, responding to negative media accounts, reads, "Prior to arriving at our destination, we passengers, accompanied and enlightened by seven naturalists, were indoctrinated again and again on preservation of the environment."[23]

Still, concern also exists over the large size of antarctic cruise ships and the potential for accidents. Any responsibility for a rescue effort would fall to nearby scientific bases and their staffs. This would be a significant disruption to their daily work, and, more importantly, their ability to rescue many people in a serious ship accident is very limited. The equipment support for a major emergency rescue operation of hundreds of people does not exist in Antarctica.

It was inevitable that scientists would study the impact of tourists in Antarctica. However, that is easier said than done. For example, it is difficult to separate the impact of tourists and scientists at the same location.

The National Science Foundation observes, "It would be prohibitively costly to attempt to monitor every site in the Antarctic Peninsula that might be subject to ship-based tourism, even if baseline information on those sites were available."[24] Nonetheless, studies are being undertaken. For example, a former British research station on the peninsula, Port Lockroy, now studies visitor impact on the resident population of gentoo penguins.

Jim Fox, a former research station base commander now working at Port Lockroy, the most popular annual peninsula tourist destination, states, "The way things work now, tourism isn't a problem. By and large the tour operators do a good job of regulating themselves. But sooner or later someone is going to try to build a hotel down here, and once that happens, answers are going to have to be found for some thorny legal and political questions we've all been putting off."[25] Furthermore, should tourists begin spending twenty-four hours a day on land, they would have as much negative impact as research bases. What the total effect of that would be on Antarctica remains to be defined.

"As yet, there is no [clear] scientific evidence of damage [by tourism] but there must be a limit to the number of visitors that sites can sustain before the vegetation or wildlife are trampled out of existence," says David Walton.[26]

Since humans cannot operate impact-free or waste-free anywhere, much less in Antarctica, the challenge is great. People must manage and limit the human impacts to minimize negative environmental effects.

3

Eye on the Minerals

SCIENTISTS BELIEVE THAT Antarctica may hold great stores of natural resources such as oil, gas, and minerals. One of the region's first explorers discovered a clue to its mineral potential. Ernest Shackleton found evidence of coal in the Transantarctic Mountains in the early 1900s. That area is now believed to contain "enormous beds of coal, perhaps the largest coalbed in the Southern Hemisphere, or even the world," according to Resources for the Future's Energy and Materials Division.[27]

A large iron deposit has been identified in the Prince Charles Mountains of East Antarctica. Some gemstones have been found on exposed antarctic beaches.

In 1973 traces of hydrocarbons, indicating oil and natural gas, were found in the continental shelf below the Ross Sea just off the antarctic coast. However, grand potential production estimates made after this find were "so speculative that they were not included in the official report of the US Geologic Survey on Antarctic Resources," notes geologist Dennis E. Hayes.[28]

The Transantarctic Mountains, some researchers feel, may contain deposits of gold, barium, manganese, lead, zinc, silver, and other minerals. Uranium may also be found in these ice-smothered antarctic peaks. The bottom rock layer of East Antarctica could contain iron and gold deposits, as well as copper and lead-zinc. The continent may well contain diamonds, and one area in West Antarctica is speculated to contain deposits of tin, platinum, and gold.

Plate Tectonics Used to Target Minerals

To help find minerals, scientists use the study of plate tectonics. With their knowledge of other continents' mineral deposits and geology, they predict what riches may lie beneath Antarctica's massive ice sheet. For example, where Australia and Antarctica used to touch millions of years ago, their mineral deposits should be similar. The Transantarctic Mountains once continued into Australia, where gold, barium, manganese, lead-zinc-silver, and other minerals have been found.

The bottom rock layer of East Antarctica resembles that underneath Africa, India, Australia, and Brazil, which have produced great iron and gold deposits as well as copper and lead-zinc. The continent may contain diamonds, which is suspected because of their presence in comparable areas of South Africa. Another area, in West Antarctica, matches with a South African deposit rich in tin, platinum, and gold. An area where hints of oil and natural gas were found in the continental shelf below Antarctica's Ross Sea used to be next to an Australian basin that now contains 2.5 billion barrels of oil and 220 cubic meters of gas.

The Antarctic Treaty, about twenty years old at the time of most of these discoveries, made no specific provisions for targeted mineral exploration or exploitation. Though no commercially viable deposit had been located by 1982, participating nations met in 1982 to devise a written framework for handling the situation.

Although the Antarctic Treaty set aside prior territorial claims, a huge and viable mineral discovery could induce countries to reassert such claims. "The treaty powers felt that rules for development would be easier to negotiate so long as nothing of commercial value had been found," science writer Deborah Shapley explains.[29] The clear intent of the negotiating parties was nonetheless that antarctic minerals would be mined eventually.

Scientists and environmentalists expressed great concern regarding the harmful environmental impacts of mining, but "many nations were unable to resist the temptation to study more seriously and scientifically such areas of potential economic interest," Shapley continues.[30] Over several years in the 1980s, as treaty nations negotiated a framework for mineral exploitation, conservation groups clamored for caution. Then a series of unrelated incidents moved the treaty nations to a dramatic change in direction.

In January 1989, an Argentine supply ship hit offshore rocks near an Antarctic Peninsula research station, spilling 250,000 gallons of diesel fuel. The spill killed numerous penguins and other seabirds and countless krill and destroyed several scientific projects set up along the coast. In the next four weeks, two separate accidents near antarctic islands, one involving a collision between a ship and an iceberg, caused additional fuel spills. Then, another four weeks later, the massive *Exxon Valdez* oil tanker spill in Alaska sent shock waves around the world.

The snow-covered Transantarctic Mountains may contain a treasure trove of minerals. Many ecologists worry about the impact mining would have on this mountain environment.

"It was incredible," remarks Susan Sabella of one environmental group. "Just like that, everything changed."[31]

New protocol bans mining

After the *Exxon Valdez* spill, Australia and France withdrew from the negotiations, and the entire Antarctica discussion soon changed from exploiting minerals to serious environmental protection. As a result, in 1991 the comprehensive document called the Protocol on Environmental Protection to the Antarctic Treaty was signed. It not only set strict environmental standards for all human activity in Antarctica but also specifically banned mining for at least fifty years.

This new protocol was a dramatic accomplishment, and environmentalists cheered its intent. Unfortunately, in just a few short years it became clear that many provisions of the agreement were not being followed. In the mid-1990s, environmentalists discovered numerous protocol violations, such as fuel depots in bird-breeding areas and chemical drums in fragile moss beds. Enforcement of the protocol provisions was proving to be more challenging than writing and signing them. Also, Antarctica's mineral potential remained a source of much discussion—and so did the resulting environmental impact of such commercial activity.

Effects of mining, drilling, and oil spills

Environmental damage inflicted by mining and drilling operations around the world is well documented. Such practices affect the air, water, soil, plants, and wildlife. The negative impact of mining could be especially devastating in the fragile antarctic environment.

Spilled oil coats the feathers of birds and the fur of animals, destroying their insulating properties and subjecting them to death by hypothermia. It can also make flying or swimming difficult, if not impossible. Animals that scavenge others or try to clean themselves end up ingesting the poisonous oil. Seabirds that have been hit by such catastrophes have been subjected to much study, as people have tried to rescue and clean them after spills.

"Bird survival will be quite different from spill to spill," explains David Jessup, veterinarian with the California Department of Fish and Game's Office of Oil Spill Prevention and Response. "The species involved, the toxicity of the oil, the weather and length of time between oiling and being picked up, all influence survival."[32]

Penguins in warmer climates have shown a better tendency than other birds for survival and rehabilitation after an oil spill, because of the layer of blubber underneath their feathers for additional insulation. Still, after an accident, nearby facilities and many people are required for quick action to clean and save birds. No such situation exists for an antarctic oil spill. "Penguin rookeries, always at the shoreline, are at risk of high losses as these birds feed in adjacent areas," explains biologist Mary Alice McWhinnie.[33]

Regarding mammals, the threat of direct contact with oil to the skin is a serious threat only to the southern fur seal, which depends on its waterproof coat for insulation. The threat to other seal species, and to whales, is mostly related to the ingestion of oil-contaminated food sources, or any resulting general reduction in marine food supply. "Such accidents have the potential of simultaneously affecting all elements and levels of the Antarctic marine ecosystem in the region of their occurrence," says McWhinnie.[34]

Antarctica's critical food source of krill, which swarms and feeds on plankton near the ocean surface, would be vulnerable to an oil spill. Though oil's specific toxicity to krill is yet unknown, as is how contaminated krill would pass it up the food chain, McWhinnie explains, "These phenomena occurring at low temperatures and in animals having low metabolic rates . . . will be different than for any animals for which such is known. Thus, whatever chemical damage results, only long time scales can be anticipated for repair or recovery."[35]

Another antarctic oil threat is a well blowout during the winter, which could flow for six months or more. Oil could not be easily burned off in the ice-clogged waters. Any spill hazard would last for years as oil froze in the winter

Far-Reaching Impact

On March 24, 1989, the catastrophic oil spill from the *Exxon Valdez* tanker into Alaska's Prince William Sound jolted people around the world. Eleven million barrels of crude oil oozed into the sea, killing thousands of birds, mammals, and fish and contaminating miles of pristine shoreline.

That ecological disaster's impact stretched all the way to the South Pole, for the *Valdez* spill may have saved Antarctica. It came just when Antarctic Treaty nations were finalizing guidelines for exploring Antarctica's mineral resources, including oil. Coupled with the impact of a few lesser oil spills that had occurred in Antarctica, the impact of the *Valdez* accident completely reversed the direction of mineral discussions. Instead of approving a document that managed mining in the region, treaty nations produced a dramatically different Protocol on Environmental Protection to the Antarctic Treaty. Among other things, this protocol banned both the exploration for, and the exploitation of, all minerals in Antarctica for fifty years.

A live guillemot is covered in oil from the Exxon Valdez *spill.*

sea ice, only to be released each spring in the thaw. Stormy seas would threaten any cleanup attempts.

Nonetheless, oil drilling off the antarctic coast represents the most likely focus of an eventual first attempt at mining the region's mineral resources. Human experiences in offshore drilling in cold regions of the Northern Hemisphere make it possible to imagine such operations in Antarctica.

Extracting ores from below Antarctica's continental ice sheet, however, would be a monumental logistical and manpower challenge, to say nothing of the cost.

"The high cost of access to the continent and most of the islands, as well as the great difficulties of operation in the offshore areas . . . will make it uneconomic to exploit any minerals but those which are high in unit value, and those only if they occur in large, rich ore bodies or fields," writes Neal Potter in his study for Resources for the Future.[36] For example, coal, sand, gravel, and iron exist in abundance in Antarctica but do not have a high enough value to justify the cost of their extraction and transport.

Any land-based mining operation must account for the fact that the surrounding ice is always moving. The top and bottom parts of a glacier do not move at the same rate. And different sections of the entire ice sheet also move at different rates. "This motion makes drilling and mining through a glacier difficult if not impossible," says researcher Ian M. Whillans.[37] For example, the United States' Amundsen–Scott South Pole station, built on one side of the Pole, will actually move across the Pole and to the other side in the near future. The surface ice at this location moves at a rate of more than thirty feet per year.

Models of antarctic mines

Before the 1991 environmental protocol and mining ban, the United States commissioned a study by Ohio State University's Institute for Polar Studies for a framework of antarctic mineral development and its possible environmental impact. The study includes hypothetical continental mining operations. One is an underground platinum mine in East Antarctica, with workers and processing plants all below the surface, and the output is sent by air to New Zealand. Another is an inland chromite mine, also underground but closer to the surface, whose output would be carried by tractor sleds some two thousand miles to a coastal port. Third is a copper, gold, and silver mine on the Antarctic Peninsula. The metals would be concentrated and refined on site and shipped directly to market. Finally, the study examines a hypothetical offshore drilling operation in the Ross Sea. All of the proposed operations carry serious environmental consequences.

Underground mines produce waste rock that must be disposed of somewhere. The warmed underground working area could disrupt the permafrost layers. Support structures and power sources, with their associated wastes, must still be constructed at the surface as for any open-pit mine. The hypothetical coastal mine would have a furnace that would expel "as much as 28 tons of sulfur dioxide a day"[38] into the atmosphere, says David H. Elliot, director of the Institute for Polar Studies at Ohio State University.

Air pollution from open-pit mining, such as that proposed for the peninsula, would pose a key problem in Antarctica. Particulates from the refineries and smelters could alter snowfall patterns. Some scientists wonder whether these particulates landing on top of the snow-covered continent could also alter the region's radiation balance. However, volcanic ash has been dispersed over large areas of Antarctica by past eruptions with no such effect, as new snowfall quickly covers up the ash.

Locally originating pollution on this scale would make it impossible for the globally targeted pollution research to continue in Antarctica—as the unspoiled laboratory for such work would have been altered forever. While the wind might disperse some waste gases, sulfur dioxide pollution of the antarctic coastal atmosphere "is considered a potentially serious problem," says ecologist Robert W. Risebrough. "The possibility exists for large-scale destruction of mosses and lichens in the vicinity of such activities."[39]

Looking North for Guidance

To help provide general clues to what effects mining and its related pollution might have in Antarctica, scientists look to what has happened in the upper Northern Hemisphere. Drilling and mining operations are active there in many areas with extremely cold temperatures and fragile ecosystems.

"In the Arctic region . . . there are very considerable areas of mineral development and hydrocarbon and gas extraction," notes David Walton of the British Antarctic Survey. "In Siberia, for example, there are enormous oil spills from fractured pipelines and heavy metal pollution problems from smelters."

Hundreds of thousands of seabirds and hundreds of seals died after the 1989 *Exxon Valdez* oil spill in Alaska. More than ten years later, oil still soils many miles of the Alaskan coastline. Some animal species have rebounded and some have not.

Fish in Alaska's Prince William Sound suffered great mortality rates after the *Valdez* spill, but many species showed little or no effects very soon after the spill. "Fish are very efficient at converting hydrocarbons they ingest into metabolites and excreting them from the liver," states Usha Varanasi, environmental conservation director of the National Oceanic and Atmospheric Administration. "Shellfish are not efficient, and we have found contaminated clams and mussels . . . from sites that were severely impacted by the spill." Nonetheless, the critical herring population crashed two years later, and no one knows why. Also, oil is still seeping into intertidal salmon spawning streams and affecting salmon fry. "The ecosystem that is there today is not the ecosystem that was there before the spill," observes Stan Senner, science coordinator for the *Exxon Valdez* Oil Spill Trustee Council.

Workers clean oil-covered rocks on the shores of Green Island, Alaska, following the Exxon Valdez *spill.*

Furthermore, the Antarctic Peninsula is bustling with wildlife, more so than anywhere else on the continent. The pollution and waste by-products of a local mine could have great impact on both the plant and animal life. At the very least, the industrial and human infrastructure required would greatly reduce or displace animal breeding grounds. "There would be very extensive to total destruction of bird rookeries and seal breeding grounds in the immediate area,"[40] notes Elliot.

Offshore drilling

These difficult land-mining issues and their high costs are why mineral interest in Antarctica returns to oil and the offshore continental shelves. In addition to the Ross Sea find in 1973, the Weddell Sea floor is suspected of harboring oil reserves. The Bellinshausen and Amundsen Sea Shelves resemble parts of South America that contain oil and gas, and the Amery Ice Shelf is near an area of sea floor that has been flagged as a potentially rich location for oil.

Still, considerable perils face antarctic oil ships or drilling rigs. These include stormy seas, moving pack ice, and huge, deadly icebergs. "The frequent occurrence of serious accidents to shipping . . . should not be underestimated because of the possible catastrophic consequences for the environment, at least in the case of oil transports," notes meteorologist Werner Schwerdtfeger. "Even the strongest ships are no more than toys in the ice around the continent."[41] In winter, when sea ice extends hundreds of miles out from the coast, underwater wells would have to be sealed. In summer, drifting pack ice and monstrous icebergs could threaten any facility on the surface or structures on a shallow ocean floor. A well very close to the shoreline could have to contend with those dangers as well as the end of a glacier cascading down from the mainland.

Underwater technology

Underwater technology has made great strides in polar applications that can offset the surface dangers presented by ice and icebergs. Small support ships can even "lasso"

icebergs and tow them away from drill ships. Also, instead of a rig extending to the surface, an entire group of wells can be connected with a "subsea completion" unit on the sea floor. To avoid the ice, submersibles can lay hundreds of miles of pipeline hundreds of meters below the surface.

Underwater drilling operations do not have to be permanent stations. A drill ship is capable of quickly disconnecting from a hole and moving away.

At this time, the true nature and extent of mineral deposits in Antarctica are unknown. The treaty bans both exploration and exploitation. Deborah Shapley notes two arguments against the existence of economically viable deposits of antarctic minerals. "One is that the continents of the Southern Hemisphere, with the exception of southernmost

Huge ice packs, like the one on which these chinstrap penguins gather, pose a constant threat to offshore drilling in the Antarctic because of the danger of collision.

Africa, have been somewhat less minerals-rich than those in the Northern Hemisphere. While this proposition may be debatable for minerals, it is nonetheless true that most giant hydrocarbon basins found to date have been in the Northern Hemisphere."[42] The second possibility is that the antarctic ice sheet may have scraped up any surface mineral deposits over millions of years and carried them out to sea as pulverized ores.

Experts note that the continent's true mineral potential, however, will ultimately be defined by (1) a specific mineral's price on the world market; and (2) the mineral's accessibility. Only a high market price would offset the extra cost of mining under Antarctica's extreme conditions and transporting over great distances.

Technological advances during the current mining ban may facilitate the "cleaner" discovery and extraction of oil or other minerals in Antarctica. Searches for alternative fuels may even reduce the need for fossil fuels. Organic weapons against pollution are being found. Microbes discovered in Australia consume toxic effluent from gold extraction. Bacteria could perform some purifying functions of smelters. Caustic red mud, itself a residue from aluminum refining, has been found to make acidic mine water drinkable. Studies show that bonemeal and seaweed can neutralize or remove heavy metal contaminants from mine tailings and water, respectively.

Still, the environmental threat from mining spills and pollution remains very real. The high cost of extracting antarctic minerals would reduce the desire to spend more dollars for pollution prevention or cleanup. Although Elliot suggests, "Regulation of mining activities would increase the probability that the levels of pollution and impacts on the environment are held down, and could promote higher standards than are known elsewhere," he admits that "even under the most tightly regulated conditions, there will be impacts on the environment and risks of unusual damage resulting from accidents."[43]

Furthermore, if and when "mineral resources of commercial value should be discovered, questions would arise

as to the rights of ownership and development," notes Paul C. Daniels.[44] Subsequent development of a contested deposit could require military protection, which would violate the Antarctic Treaty ban against military activities. So the politics of mining in Antarctica are just as much a concern as the logistics and effects. These are the issues that must be wrestled with as the treaty ban on mining approaches possible review in the mid–twenty-first century.

Members of an oil-drilling platform prepare to tow away an enormous iceberg that threatens to crash into the rig.

4

A Changing Climate

ONE OF THE most important scientific studies in Antarctica is that of climate. The continent's own unique combination of varying factors, such as temperature, precipitation, sunlight, and ice, forms a complex weather system. Furthermore, what happens there can affect weather all over the planet. The cold water currents flowing northward from Antarctica reach all over the world, influencing the weather of oceans and, in turn, landmasses. A significant change in the nature of those currents would have worldwide impact. Scientists have recently linked the global El Niño and La Niña weather patterns with weather in Antarctica.

Not only do researchers compile and study local weather statistics, they also work to gather and archive data about Antarctica's climate history. This will help to establish a range of climate parameters within which variations can be expected in the future. This is important for determining whether the climate today or that of the future is historically unusual for the region.

Because the temperature of Antarctica has been rising in recent years, that particular component of climate receives a great deal of attention. In particular, three large-scale local impacts of warming have been monitored. All of them introduce domino-effect changes into the ecosystem. First, because warm air translates into warmer water temperatures at the ocean surface, there is now less sea ice in the winter. A second significant change is that warmer air holds more water, which results in more precipitation or snowfall. Third, warmer air and water mean more, or faster, melting of Antarctica's glaciers and ice shelves.

British Antarctic Survey meteorologist John Turner notes, "In recent decades we've seen a complex picture of temperature change on the whole Antarctic continent. Whilst the Antarctic Peninsula region has seen one of the largest temperature increases on Earth over the last 50 years, the South Pole has experienced a small cooling. However, what we can say is that Antarctica is extremely sensitive to environmental change."[45]

Less sea ice

Away from Antarctica's coast, the South Pole temperatures have remained fairly stable, and occasionally have been colder than recent times. Where Antarctica is warming,

 ### How Antarctica Affects Global Climate

Global climates are most directly affected by the formation of sea ice around Antarctica. Sea ice increases the amount of solar radiation reflected back into space versus what would be reflected by open water. Consequently, changes in the extent of sea ice can change the amount of heat entering the atmosphere, which in turn affects climate. Sea ice also shields the ocean from wind and the wind's influence on ocean circulation.

Antarctic bottom water, cold salty water formed around Antarctica as a result of sea ice formation, is a major component of the world's ocean circulation system. This water circulates from Antarctica all the way into the Northern Hemisphere over periods of decades or longer. The temperature of this water and its interaction with the air and other surrounding water affect the climate in these areas. A small change in the wind or temperature at the surface of the Southern Ocean around Antarctica may alter the rate of production of antarctic bottom water. This, in turn, may change the deep-water circulation of the oceans, thereby altering the world's climate in a potentially significant way.

however, is where much of its wildlife seeks food, shelter, and breeding grounds—along the coast, the peninsula, and antarctic islands. That is where the documented loss of sea ice appears to be having the broadest impact.

Over the last fifty years, warmer winters have produced less sea ice, with average winter temperatures on the peninsula rising by nearly ten degrees Fahrenheit. Since sea ice can as much as double the size of Antarctica, a reduction in that volume would have a significant impact on the ecosystem. Decades ago, extensive sea ice formed three or four out of every five winters. Today, this occurs only once or twice every five years. Algae grow on the underside of this ice, which in turn feed krill, the number one food source for antarctic wildlife. Without sea ice in the spawning grounds, each new generation of krill dies. This has led to a lower wildlife survival rate among the dependents on krill, especially for the fragile young.

"No ice means no food for the krill," says Wayne Trivelpiece, director of seabird research for the U.S. Antarctic Marine Living Resources program (USAMLR). "What we are seeing here is the first evidence of how a shift in climate may have a surprisingly quick and dramatic impact."[46]

The emperor penguin is considered the species most vulnerable to a warming climate. Major fluctuations in populations in the Ross Sea region, where 30 percent of the world's emperors breed, indicate how dependent the birds are on extensive, reliable sea ice. Population increases were recorded in the 1990s where sea ice was dependable; drops were noted where it was not. One well-studied emperor penguin population has dropped by 50 percent in the last fifty years.

Less sea ice has contributed greatly, as well, to Adelie penguin population declines. Adelie populations studied on five islands near Palmer Station on the peninsula have plunged 40 percent in the last twenty-five years. Six colonies have gone extinct. Further distressing scientists is that fewer young krill are found in penguin diets, indicating that krill are not breeding successfully either. The last successful breeding year for krill in the area was 1995.

Since the maximum life span of krill is about six years, a critical time is approaching. Also declining are chinstrap penguins. While chinstraps like the open water that less sea ice provides, the resulting lack of krill in those waters has had an effect.

"During the past 10 years we have seen a sharp decline in the survival rate of penguin chicks," Trivelpiece continues. "With so few krill close by, they have to swim out farther and longer in search of food, making themselves easy snacks for leopard seals."[47]

The availability of krill to sustain Antarctic wildlife is critical. "We're really on the wire right now," Trivelpiece explained during the 2001 Antarctic winter. "If we don't get ice this winter or next, the whole house of cards will come down."[48]

Less sea ice also affects the heat exchange in the atmosphere. Without it, more heat is absorbed at the Earth's surface rather than reflected back into space.

Researchers have attributed declining Adelie penguin populations to the effects of global warming on the Antarctic.

More precipitation

Increased snowfall from the warmer air threatens the Adelies on the peninsula, which depend on exposed, rocky areas for nesting. With more snow covering the ground, the penguins lose many eggs and chicks in depressions that

 ### Home of the Blizzard

Australian explorer Doug Mawson's harrowing antarctic expedition of 1912–1913 remains one of the world's great adventure stories. His team unknowingly set up its coastal base of operations in one of Antarctica's windiest, most brutal locations. The horrific, never-ending winds left as much a mark on the men as any of their other experiences on the frozen continent. Here is just one paragraph from Mawson's book, *Home of the Blizzard:*

> The climate proved to be little more than one continuous blizzard the year round; a hurricane of wind roaring for weeks together, pausing for breath only at odd hours. Such pauses—lulls of a singular nature—were a welcome relief to the dreary monotony, and on such occasions the auditory sense was strangely affected. The contrast was so severe when the [w]racking gusts of an abating wind suddenly gave way to intense, eerie silence that the habitual droning of many weeks would still reverberate in the ears. At night one would involuntarily wake up if the wind died away and be loath to sleep for "the hunger of a sound."

Doug Mawson led a harrowing Antarctic expedition in 1912.

turn into slush. Making matters worse, a smaller breeding colony is at greater risk for even more losses to skuas, predatory birds that steal chicks and eggs.

Plant life and microorganisms could benefit from the warming and added precipitation, spreading their territories. Higher temperatures, combined with greater precipitation and meltwater, make conditions more hospitable for them. Expansion of plants on the Antarctic Peninsula has been documented from 1990 to 2000. On the other hand, some plants especially adapted to the cold and dry air may not adapt well to the warmer temperatures and increased precipitation. They could be overtaken by the ones that do.

Warmer temperatures have affected the ecosystem of lakes on some antarctic islands. Frozen lakes studied on Signy Island northeast of the Antarctic Peninsula have seen an increase of ice-free summer days by as much as a month in the last twenty years. As a result, lake temperatures have risen further because of the increase in solar energy absorbed. This, combined with more nutrient-rich meltwater flowing into the lakes, has resulted in an increase of phosphate and a flourishing algae population. The amount of chlorophyll in the lakes has risen 300 percent, just from a temperature change of about two degrees Fahrenheit.

However, those dramatic changes and impacts are not occurring throughout Antarctica. In other parts of the continent, the climate has stayed much the same. Along part of the Ross Ice Shelf near Cape Crozier, the sea ice has grown in recent years to the benefit of resident penguin populations. Some ice streams feeding the Ross Ice Shelf are deeper and are moving slower than in recent decades. The so-called Dry Valleys have seen a drop in average temperatures. The average surface temperature of the antarctic continent is still well below zero, with no melting occurring most places at any time of the year.

Giant icebergs and melting ice shelves

Although some penguin colonies had been thriving near Cape Crozier, they are now threatened by another menace—giant icebergs breaking off the ice shelf. The Ross Ice Shelf recently spawned huge icebergs more than one thousand square miles in size, which drifted near the penguins' breeding sites and isolated them from the sea in the spring of 2001. The icebergs created a barrier that altered winds and ocean current patterns. Sheltered from storms, the sea ice extended well beyond its normal range and cut off penguins from their breeding areas. Able to walk at only 1 mile per hour, versus swimming at 4.5 miles per hour, the penguins were severely distanced from food because of the longer walk across sea ice. This problem grew in 2002 and even threatened human access to the nearby McMurdo base.

One small colony of twelve hundred emperor penguins in the area failed to raise any chicks. A small Adelie colony at nearby Cape Royds, the longest-studied in Antarctica, will "fail totally,"[49] claims researcher David Ainley. This southernmost Adelie colony, situated next to a hut built by explorer Ernest Shackleton in the early 1900s, has been monitored annually since 1959.

Much attention has been focused on this proliferation of super icebergs as a further sign of serious global warming. The icebergs are so large that news reports compare them to American states in size.

In March 2000, an iceberg measuring 185 miles long and 23 miles wide broke off the Ross Ice Shelf in West Antarctica. At 4,200 square miles, it is just smaller than the state of Connecticut. Named "B-15," it is the largest iceberg ever reliably measured. B-15 is about a quarter-mile thick, but only one hundred feet of that is visible above water.

It is thought that B-15 represents the giant calving of the Ross Ice Shelf expected every fifty to one hundred years—not necessarily a sign of global warming. In contrast, the smaller Larsen and Wilkins Ice Shelves around the Antarctic Peninsula have been dramatically breaking up for nearly ten years. One of the biggest incidents came in 1995, when more than five hundred square miles of the Larsen Ice Shelf fell apart.

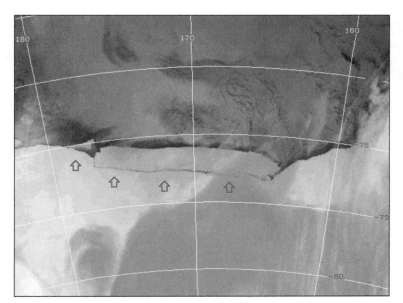

A satellite image shows the gigantic iceberg (indicated by arrows) created when an edge of the Ross Ice Shelf broke in March, 2000.

David Vaughan of the British Antarctic Survey notes, "They are not calving big, healthy, periodic bergs like B-15, and that is the whole point. It is not business as usual."[50]

The crumbling ice at Larsen and Wilkins cannot be explained only by recent rising temperatures, because the thick ice cannot soften that fast. It is believed that the warmer peninsula temperatures also cause melt pools to form on the ice shelves' surfaces. This meltwater percolates down into the ice shelf and forms crevasses. When a number of crevasses reach down to sea level, seawater rushes in and refreezes, which blows the ice apart. In March 2002, another section of the Larsen Ice Shelf—as big as Rhode Island—broke up.

"The reason this is worth paying attention to is that we're seeing a very rapid and profound response by the ice sheet to a warming that's been around for just a few years," remarks Ted Scambos of the National Snow and Ice Data Center.[51]

Vaughan agrees. "We knew what was left would collapse eventually, but the speed of it is staggering. Hard to believe that 500 million billion tons of ice sheet has disintegrated in less than a month."[52]

From Forests to Freezing

Antarctica has not always been frozen. Once a forested, semi-tropical land, it was part of a larger supercontinent that slowly separated into the continents we know today. In fact, studies in Antarctica support the theories of continental drift now commonly accepted.

In the 1800s several scientists suggested that Earth's continents were once joined. This could explain why plants and fossils among distant lands are so similar. In 1912 Alfred Wegener proposed the first complete theory of this continental drift. He called the original giant continent Pangaea ("all lands") and hypothesized that all of today's continents came from it.

However, since Wegener could not explain how or why the continents separated, his idea was scorned by much of the world's scientific community. Furthermore, comparable climates could explain similarities in plant and animal life on separate continents. And to suggest that the continents' shapes appear to fit together—like puzzle pieces—seemed childishly simplistic.

Then exploration of the sea floor in the mid-1900s led geologist H.H. Hess to his theory of plate tectonics. He saw that the various sections of the ocean floors were slowly spreading away from each other, with the major intersections of plates occurring underwater. This gave Wegener's theory the drift mechanism it had lacked. Scientists soon found fossils in Antarctica that included a deciduous tree, a fern, a terrestrial reptile, and a small mammal. Later, dinosaur bones were discovered there. These were all consistent with the fossils and climates of earlier South America, Africa, India, and Australia. Antarctica's secrets proved that Wegener and Hess were both correct.

Just two months after the Larsen breakup, in May 2002, the Ross Ice Shelf calved another giant iceberg, this one larger than Delaware—or about twenty-five hundred square miles. These events have drawn dire predictions from some circles that global warming will melt the ice sheets of Antarctica and flood the world's coastlines. Others point out that these icebergs and ice shelves of recent news reports were already floating—thus their breaking off or crumbling has not displaced any more seawater or affected sea levels.

Still, the dramatic loss of ice seems to be mostly limited to the Antarctic Peninsula area. This region is closest to the equator, and its climate is further moderated by the sea sur-

Two hundred million years ago, all of the southern continents were indeed joined together, along with India. Slowly they drifted apart; India headed north to ultimately slam into Asia (creating the Himalaya Mountains) and Antarctica moved south. Africa, South America, and Australia spread out along the Southern Hemisphere. By 40 million years ago, Antarctica neared the bottom of the Earth and began to dramatically cool. Snow and ice took over completely about 7 million years ago. The final proof of continental drift lay underneath Antarctica's ice.

Specifically, eastern South America used to abut western Africa. India and Antarctica fit beside the east side of Africa. Southern Australia wrapped around one edge of Antarctica. And the southern tip of South America touched the northern tip of the Antarctic Peninsula—simple, but true.

An illustration shows the Earth two hundred million years ago when all continents were joined, forming Pangaea.

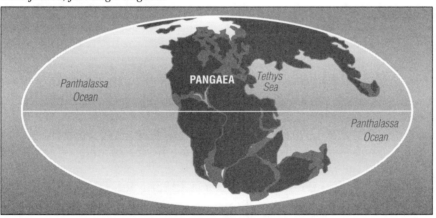

rounding it on three sides. The documented temperature increases there over the last fifty years are not matched anywhere else on the continent. When compared with the peninsula, the rest of Antarctica's stability of climate over the last several decades is remarkable.

Cycles of warming

Broader-timed research is showing that the antarctic region has experienced periods of significant warming and cooling over tens of thousands of years. Analysis of ocean-floor sediments drilled from around the Antarctic Peninsula indicates that the current ice shelves may be only two thousand years old. "The current rate of warming may be unusual, but our research shows definitively that [the peninsula] has been warm and ice-free at times in the past few thousand years,"[53] says geologist Carol Pudsey of the British Antarctic Survey.

Thus, while it is true that so-called greenhouse gases released into the atmosphere can affect temperatures somewhat, the overall effect of those gases may be small in comparison with the larger forces of nature. If the peninsula ice shelves have already come and gone at least once since the last ice age—about eleven thousand years ago—it is hard to lay all the blame on mankind for what is going on now.

"We've got a sedimentary record that reveals very significant changes in water temperature and ice melt during the past 7,000 years," explains Robert Dunbar of Stanford University. "The cause of these highly variable climate changes is still a mystery."[54]

Dunbar's research shows that from 5,000 to 7,000 years ago, regular cycles of warming and cooling in West Antarctica lasted 400, 200, 140, and 70 years. "We believe these cycles of warming and cooling may have been caused by variations in the amount of energy emitted by the sun,"[55] he says.

Research on the East Antarctic ice sheet shows that it has advanced and retreated for as long as a million years. Studies on the West Antarctic ice sheet indicate that it extended hundreds of miles farther out into the ocean thousands of years ago, and began a long, slow retreat then—rather than in the last fifty years. Specifically, the grounding line of the ice sheet—where the bottom of the ice shelf still touches the ocean floor—has retreated eight hundred miles over that period. That represents a move of about four hundred feet per year for the last seventy-six hundred years.

"Collapse appears to be part of an ongoing natural cycle, probably caused by the rising sea level initiated by the melting of the Northern Hemisphere ice sheets at the end of the last ice age," remarks Howard Conway of the University of Washington. "Global warming could speed the process."[56]

If the West Antarctic ice sheet were to melt completely, it could raise the global sea level by fifteen to twenty feet, but would take seven thousand years to do so. The current melting rate raises the sea level by about an inch every twenty-five years. If all of Antarctica's ice were to melt, the sea level would rise much more than that, but continental temperatures would have to rise dozens of degrees to initiate such a phenomenon.

Studies of the Fimbul Ice Shelf on Antarctica's Princess Martha coast show it retreating in some places and advancing in others. This interests scientists because it lies at the same latitude as collapsing ice shelves on the Antarctic Peninsula. Since the Fimbul Ice Shelf is not dramatically breaking up like those on the peninsula, latitude cannot be the only factor.

Researcher Kenneth Jezek of Ohio State University's Byrd Polar Research Center summarizes, "There are mixed signals almost everywhere you turn, with little consistent pattern. That's why it is important to measure ice movement in many different places at different times, to gauge overall effects."[57]

The ozone hole

Another climate-related phenomenon studied in Antarctica is the much-publicized "ozone hole" that occurs every spring in the continent's upper atmosphere. A chemical reaction, caused primarily by man-made chlorofluorocarbons that add chlorine and bromine to the upper atmosphere, destroys ozone in the air. The hole has grown larger than North America (10 million square miles) in recent years. The critical ozone layer of the Earth's atmosphere absorbs harmful ultraviolet-B (UV-B) radiation from the sun. When there is no ozone to absorb it, the radiation passes all the way down to the Earth's surface, where it can cause skin and eye problems and other disorders.

This annual occurrence is greatest over Antarctica compared with other regions because of the extremely cold temperatures in the stratosphere. The reemergence of sunlight after a long, dark winter triggers the reaction, which

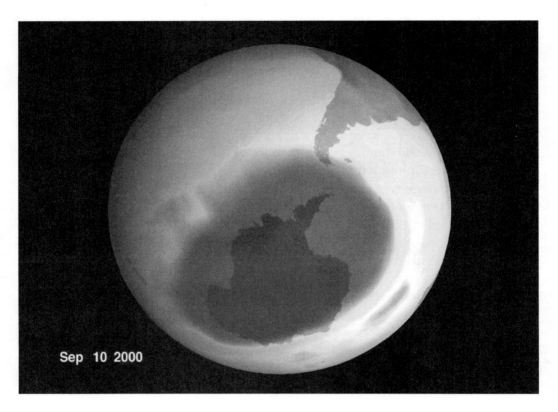

Sep 10 2000

NASA recorded a satellite image of a 10-million-square-mile hole in the ozone over Antarctica in 2000. This hole allows dangerous ultraviolet radiation from the sun to reach the Earth.

lasts well into the summer. Although the offending synthetic chemicals were banned during the late twentieth century (they were popular in aerosol sprays, refrigerants, plastic foams, and fire extinguishers), their life span in the atmosphere is twenty to one hundred years. Thinning ozone on a smaller scale has been detected over other areas of the world.

In 1997 the first direct evidence of UV-B damage to animal DNA was discovered. Scientists studying the Antarctic icefish found DNA lesions in its eggs and larvae. "It is striking how closely the damage to the fish eggs tracked with the increased intensity of ultraviolet light," notes William Detrich of Northeastern University.[58]

Such damage can occur in algae and the krill that feed upon them, which could affect the entire antarctic food chain. Most antarctic plant species and some animal species have natural UV-B filters for protection.

"Since the entire Antarctic food web is driven by the annual bloom in phytoplankton productivity that occurs in spring and summer, any major impact on these microscopic plants and bacterioplankton by increased ultraviolet radiation levels in spring could have implications for the entire marine ecosystem," warns one scientific assessment.[59]

Recent research indicates that the ozone hole may be contributing to Antarctica's climate changes. Effects from the ozone hole create atmospheric changes that would be consistent with the warming of the Antarctic Peninsula and the simultaneous cooling of other areas, especially in East Antarctica.

Most scientists predict that the early twenty-first century should bring the peak of the ozone hole's size, followed by a gradual decline for the next few decades as the chemical levels in the stratosphere subside. Indeed, the hole in 2000 was the largest ever, but it opened early and collapsed

Scientists release a balloon into the atmosphere over the Antarctic that will measure the levels of ozone layer.

quickly. In 2001 the hole was about 10 percent smaller. Still, while emissions of ozone-depleting chemicals into the atmosphere are dropping, stratospheric concentrations of the chemicals are increasing because of the long air-borne lives of the substances.

The ozone hole, radiation levels, and their effects will be closely monitored from now on. With Antarctica's weather inescapably linked to the entire world's climate, changes on the frozen continent are almost universally considered to be potential precursors to similar developments worldwide.

5

Vigilance for Antarctica

PROTECTING THE ANTARCTIC environment from the threats it now faces will take knowledge, resources, and commitment: knowledge of what the threats are and how to meet them; the financial and human resources to carry out programs to squelch or reduce the threats; and the commitment by people and countries all over the world to create and follow through on protection and management programs.

The mechanism that may give people the best chance for success in protecting Antarctica was created more than forty years ago, before such knowledge or resources even existed. It was created at a time when the countless treasures Antarctica held were yet unknown, but many nations were eager to discover what the continent held in store.

As a result of this intense interest in Antarctica, controversy had been brewing in the 1950s. Seven countries had made territorial claims and set up bases to support those claims. The United States already had held military exercises there to prepare troops and equipment for extreme fighting conditions. The nations had to organize and cooperate.

Fortunately, the world's scientists convened an International Geophysical Year in 1958 to aggressively address the emerging exploration of two new frontiers—outer space and Antarctica. Sponsored by the International Council of Scientific Unions, the project involved eighteen months of work by scientists from sixty-seven countries in a variety of disciplines. The effort was deemed a rousing success. It inspired twelve nations to meet biweekly for seven months at the National Science Foundation (NSF) in Washington, D.C., to devise an effective political framework for the frozen continent's future. This thoughtful dialogue produced a precedent-setting agreement.

Antarctic treaty

Known as the Antarctic Treaty, this ground breaking document established a framework to protect the continent from chaos and regulate its day-to-day use. It is now recognized as one of the most successful international agreements ever negotiated.

The treaty was signed in 1959 and fully ratified in 1961 by Argentina, Australia, Belgium, Chile, France, Japan, New Zealand, Norway, South Africa, the Soviet Union, the United Kingdom, and the United States of America.

Several countries plant their flags at the South Pole to signify the international agreement to utilize and explore the Antarctic responsibly.

The document puts on hold any territorial claims without disputing them or recognizing them. Other basic tenets include the prohibition of military bases or exercises or weapons testing; the banning of nuclear testing and radioactive waste disposal; the free exchange of scientific information; and the free access to any antarctic areas, stations, ships, or planes by treaty participants (with advance notice). In short, Antarctica was preserved for peace and science.

"The Antarctic Treaty is given high marks for its success in mandating demilitarization and denuclearization of the area," says international law expert Christopher C. Joyner, "as well as in promoting free scientific research and cooperation and peaceful settlement of disputes."[60]

All land and ice shelves below sixty degrees south latitude are covered by the treaty. Sixteen more nations signed on later and became active in scientific research there. Joining the original twelve treaty signers were Brazil, Bulgaria, China, Ecuador, Finland, Germany, India, Italy, Korea, Peru, Poland, Spain, Sweden, Ukraine, and Uruguay. More than a dozen other countries have since "recognized" the agreement, with the declared intent to pursue research and eventually become full treaty participants.

The success of this Antarctic Treaty system over the last forty years is held up as inspiration for other international negotiations. Today twenty-five countries operate dozens of bases on the continent and about twenty surrounding islands. The continent's winter population exceeds one thousand, and the summer population approaches ten thousand. The United States operates a year-round station at the South Pole (Amundsen–Scott South Pole station) and bases in several other locations around Antarctica.

Environmental protection

Still, the main treaty was just a start. The first treaty amendment, passed in 1964, specifies measures to protect Antarctica's plants and animals and to allow for "Specially Protected Areas" and "Sites of Special Scientific Interest." In 1978 another document was enacted to regulate sealing

The entrance to the dome at Amundsen–Scott South Pole station. This is the United States' year-round research station in the Antarctic.

activities, protecting three species and limiting access to others. A 1980 measure regulates activity in the southern ocean surrounding Antarctica, especially relating to the commercial exploitation of krill, the primary food source for marine animals.

In the late 1980s, serious interest in Antarctica's potential mineral deposits developed. Coal had been discovered in the interior mountains; oil was believed to lie under the sea floor. Various governments seemed prepared to use the treaty's official thirty-year review date of 1991 as an avenue for exploitation. Other groups opposed the idea. Then the oil spill disaster of the *Exxon Valdez* hit Alaska in 1989. Overwhelming pressure against mineral extraction arose, and as a result a new protocol was passed banning the mining of antarctic resources for at least fifty years. Furthermore, it sets up Antarctica as a "natural reserve," establishes environmental principles for all activities, and subjects all activities to a prior assessment of their environmental impact. This document is called the Protocol on Environmental Protection to the Antarctic Treaty.

The treaty and its protocols provide guidelines for the environmental protection of Antarctica, but they are not always followed. Countries are on a kind of honor system of compliance; no regular, ongoing program of code enforcement exists. Increasing research, growing tourism, interest in mineral resources, and global warming/ozone depletion are all poised to degrade the antarctic environment in the twenty-first century. The future of Antarctica is not set, and the human race stands on the threshold of another era of challenge to protect the great frozen continent.

Antarctic Treaty nations meet regularly to discuss whatever issues face the region and mankind's presence there. Protecting the environment from a variety of threats has become an important part of that discussion. Significant attention is finally being paid to pollution, both past and present, at research bases. Nations are looking at ways to clean up forty years of garbage and implementing programs to minimize further pollution.

Cleaning up

In 1985 Australia closed its antarctic landfills and committed to a cleanup program that has now removed waste from most of its sites. A new operation is expected to clean up more than three thousand tons of waste at Australia's Casey station. In the 1986–1987 summer season, the United States sent one cargo ship with seventeen hundred tons of waste home for recycling or disposal. The following year, the NSF outlined a $30 million, four-year cleanup plan for American bases in Antarctica.

Throughout the 1990s, the United States and New Zealand invested resources in cleaning up and removing contamination at past and current research sites. The U.S. Antarctic Program has a team dedicated to such tasks at McMurdo station, the Dry Valleys, the Ross Ice Shelf, and other locations. New Zealand's closed Hallett station has been significantly cleaned up, and penguins have retaken their breeding grounds there (though scientists say more cleanup is needed).

During the summer of 2000–2001, the British Antarctic Survey began a four-year program to remove Britain's

The Antarctic Treaty System

Signed in 1959 and effective starting in 1961, the original Antarctic Treaty features fourteen articles defining the continent as a place for science and peace, with no territorial claims by countries. Participating nations meet on an annual basis to discuss the management of antarctic affairs and additions to the treaty. Since 1961 additional annexes, conventions, and recommendations have been added to what is now known as the Antarctic Treaty system. Four major additions to the treaty further establish rules for the management of the continent's ecosystem:

Agreed Measures for the Conservation of Antarctic Fauna and Flora (1964)—Protects all native plants and animals, including special protection for Ross seals and fur seals, and allows the designation of Specially Protected Areas and Sites of Special Scientific Interest.

Convention for the Conservation of Antarctic Seals (1978)—Framework to regulate commercial sealing, if it were to resume (unlikely). Totally protects three species (Ross, elephant, and fur) and sets catch limits for others.

Convention on the Conservation of Antarctic Marine Living Resources (1980)—Although negotiated under the Antarctic Treaty, covers area larger than that by including the entire ecosystem south of the Southern Ocean's Antarctic Convergence. Protects the marine food supply of all of Antarctica's wildlife, especially krill, by prohibiting overfishing.

Protocol on Environmental Protection to the Antarctic Treaty (1991)—Prohibits mining and prospecting for at least fifty years, subjects all activities to prior environmental impact assessments, and establishes detailed environmental principles for all activities conducted there.

abandoned bases and waste dumps. More than 1 million English pounds funded the start of this cleanup, with a final cost of nearly 4 million pounds (about $6.6 million) expected by 2005. France and South Africa have launched cleanup operations as well.

In addition to cleaning up, scientists are finding ways to reduce pollution in their current operations. The waste produced at many sites is now treated, recycled, and/or removed as a requirement to operate there.

Australia has installed small sewage treatment plants at all of its stations. Plans are being made to install sewage treatment facilities at the McMurdo station and Scott Base in the Ross Sea area. All solid wastes generated at McMurdo are now removed to the United States. Solid waste from the Amundsen–Scott South Pole station is taken to McMurdo for ultimate removal. New Zealand also removes all of its solid waste from Antarctica. (In the past, sewage was dumped into the sea, and solid waste was incinerated or discarded onto sea ice or open land dumps.)

Personnel with specific environmental assignments and responsibilities operate routinely at many research sites. All scientific activities are watched closely for their effect on the environment, and environmental impact assessments are made. At Australian bases, for example, each station leader is responsible

In an effort to keep pollution and waste at a minimum in the Antarctic, large amounts of trash are compacted into cubes.

for environmental management and is assisted by the station environment committee, a station environmental officer, and a station waste management officer.

Strict procedures also apply to workers who travel far from bases to conduct research, pointed out Robert Rutford, a geologist and antarctic researcher, in a report to Congress.

> The scientists who go into the field now return all waste, including human waste from land and ablation areas. Old camp sites that are visited are cleaned up, flares that are used to make landing sites are carefully recovered, and other items that may have been left in the past are marked for future pickup. The scientific community has bought into the Environmental Protocol in a meaningful way. The special funds that Congress provided to the NSF made what looked like an impossible task, possible, and what you see at McMurdo and other U.S. stations is something we can all take pride in.[61]

Alternative energy sources offer hope for reducing the amount of fossil fuels needed to power and heat bases.

A group of scientists stands alongside a solar panel which is used as an alternative to fossil fuel in powering research facilities in the Antarctic.

This will reduce greenhouse gas emissions, as well as fuel spills. New modular power systems for antarctic bases now provide cleaner, more efficient energy. One such system uses solar and wind power, storing energy in batteries. This minimizes the use of petroleum fuels and makes logical use of Antarctica's fierce winds and twenty-four-hour summer daylight. The Australian Antarctic Division is helping to develop a powerful wind turbine system to eliminate the need for diesel fuel at several research stations. A new sixteen-person station at Sweden's antarctic base features triple-glazed windows to regulate and ventilate heat, solar electricity panels, and a heat exchanger to circulate air.

This cleanup effort and drive for cleaner energy is uneven, however, as each country determines what resources it has to commit and its timetable for doing so. Some countries have relatively limited resources, and in 2002 Russia was considered to be on the brink of shutting down its entire antarctic program. Russia once operated the most extensive network of bases, but with the breakup of the Soviet Union came a shortage of money. The Environmental Protocol requires countries to clean up and remove abandoned bases, a huge task that would "cost Russia $120 million and take almost 10 years to accomplish,"[62] according to the Russian newspaper *Pravda*. If it had that amount of money for such an effort, Russia could afford to keep its antarctic program alive.

Tourism

New technology will no doubt continue to flow into Antarctica, providing more efficient operations and less fossil fuel pollution. But joining this march to the frozen continent will also be an increasing number of tourists, and with them will come more environmental pressure. While in the 1990s the rise in tourism in Antarctica coincided with the serious attention paid to environmental issues, there are still concerns about the growing volume of commercial travel there.

The consensus is that ships will remain the primary commercial mode of tourist travel in Antarctica, and demand

Because cruise ships, like the one pictured, deliver thousands of visitors to the Antarctic every year, scientists have begun to more closely study the impact of tourism on this region.

will continue to grow. The visitor count topped fifteen thousand in the 2001–2002 summer and is predicted to reach twenty-five thousand per summer within the next four years. The islands and Antarctic Peninsula will remain the most sought-after destinations. A slight but unpredictable increase is expected for adventure tourism and air travel.

Although the high costs of the tours and the limited number of tour operators will restrain growth somewhat, larger cruise ships will make Antarctica more economical for sightseers. While the majority of antarctic vessels carry relatively few total passengers, major cruise lines have recently taken about one thousand or more passengers each through the Southern Ocean in the last few years. These large ships cruise the islands and the Antarctic Peninsula without putting passengers ashore. The International Association for Antarctic Travel Operators (IAATO) expanded its membership categories in 2001 to accommodate such large ships, as well as "fly-in" operations that deliver tourists to ships waiting for them in Antarctica—a program currently targeted by Chile at King George Island.

The Protocol for Environmental Protection to the Antarctic Treaty provides general guidelines for tourism, and the IAATO emphasizes adherence to these principles, but there are many details and issues that have not been fully addressed, as well as a general lack of knowledge about many locations.

To help monitor this increased activity and further develop environmental guidelines, the Environmental Protocol established the Antarctic Site Inventory project. The program is intended to collect data on the impact of visitors in specific areas. Started in 1994, the project began assessing the existing facts about, and status of, the most popular antarctic sites. Visitor traffic and environmental impact will be closely monitored. In the project's first six years, personnel made 287 visits to fifty-nine sites in the peninsula area. Over time, this program will give all parties a better understanding of how to deal with increasing numbers of visitors.

Despite concerns about the volume of tourism, many antarctic experts agree that these visitors could help increase the number of ambassadors for the continent's continued protection. Antarctic travel expert Thomas Bauer explains, "If it were not for tourism, some argue, many national parks would never have been established and animal species . . . would not be protected from exploitation. Likewise, numerous remote and relatively pristine places on the globe would not be protected if it were not for the desire of travelers to visit such sites."[63]

Although no overnight facilities yet exist on land for tourists, such developments are still a possibility if they were to be designed within antarctic environmental guidelines. Again, high costs and a short travel season have thus far kept such ideas on the drawing board. Still, the Antarctic and Southern Oceans Coalition (ASOC) decried the IAATO's expansion of membership categories and in 2001

Travel Operators' Code of Conduct

The International Association of Antarctic Tour Operators publishes a code of conduct required of all of its travelers. It focuses on issues contained in the Antarctic Treaty system and has seven main directives:

1. Do not disturb, harass, or interfere with the wildlife.
2. Do not walk on or otherwise damage the fragile plants, i.e., lichens, mosses, and grasses.
3. Leave nothing behind, and take only memories and photographs.
4. Do not interfere with protected areas or scientific research.
5. Historic huts may only be entered when accompanied by a properly authorized escort.
6. Do not smoke during shore excursions.
7. Stay with your group or with one of the ship's leaders when ashore.

The Antarctic Treaty's Recommendation XVIII-1 under the Environmental Protocol goes into even greater detail and includes specific guidelines for tour operators on how to coordinate and interact with national authorities at scientific bases and how to follow the environmental rules of the treaty.

called for a limit on antarctic tourists. "This is justified in order to protect the natural values and political stability of the region,"[64] claimed the ASOC proposal. The IAATO responded by indicating that these other tourist programs were going to happen anyway, and therefore it would be better to have them operating under the existing operators' environmentally sensitive regulatory system.

Another thorny issue arose in the 2001–2002 summer when a French research base tried to tax an Australian tourist ship that landed at its location. According to the Antarctic Treaty, no land claims can be advanced and all research sites are open to visitors who give advance notice.

While most national program managers in Antarctica have established restrictions on station visits to minimize the impact on station operations and personnel, no one had ever tried to levy a tax before. "Very important issues are at stake and will I am sure be addressed by other Antarctic Treaty partners," remarked trip leader Don McIntyre. "Certainly the IAATO is most concerned about this development and will be seeking clarification in the future."[65]

Illegal fishing

One area where the Treaty's protections are not working is in restrictions on fishing in the Southern Ocean. The Convention on the Conservation of Antarctic Marine Living Resources (1980) attempts to protect the region from overfishing by setting catch limits and other guidelines. Great concern exists about depleting the region's marine food supply and the killing of antarctic seabirds. Illegal fishing operations outside the scope of these guidelines were still rampant in 2001–2002, and seabird kills on long-line hooks were at an all-time high. A Catch Document System, designed under the Antarctic Treaty in 1999 to provide a paper trail to catch pirate fishers, has instead been used to launder the illegal catches. The Australian Navy commandeered three illegal fishing ships in February 2002 and arrested a notorious ringleader of the international trade of toothfish (sometimes called Chilean sea bass) from Antarctica.

Antarctic Treaty parties will have to continue to work to find a way to stop the depletion of food sources in the Southern Ocean. In the meantime, a public boycott of the toothfish grew in the spring of 2002. The boycott uses prominent chefs and U.S. restaurants, who remove the item from their menus. Called "Take a Pass on Chilean Sea Bass," the program includes more than 150 chefs and restaurants in San Francisco, Philadelphia, and Chicago, with additions expected in New York, Los Angeles, and Washington, D.C., among other cities. The campaign also asks consumers to refrain from ordering the product at restaurants that serve it.

Climate change and ozone

A much broader fight is being waged in the realm of global warming. While local programs in Antarctica promote reduction in fuel emissions there, the continent cannot escape the effects of the greater volume of greenhouse gases put into the atmosphere by the world's other six continents.

Governments from around the world are working to enact programs and laws to reduce the amount of greenhouse gases emitted from power plants and cars. In 1992 the United Nations created the Framework Convention on Climate Change, seeking to reduce destructive chemical emissions, and in 1997 added the Kyoto Protocol. This protocol requires industrialized nations to reduce their emissions of greenhouse gases to pre-1990 levels by 2012. However, the protocol is binding only on nations that ratify it, a process that has taken years and is still not complete. About seventy nations such as Japan and the fifteen

A group of demonstrators protests the United States' refusal to sign the Kyoto Protocol climate pact in 2002.

countries of the European Union had ratified Kyoto by the summer of 2002, but important countries like the United States, Australia, China, India, and Russia had not. The future of the Kyoto Protocol is therefore unclear, and the possibility of increasing global levels of greenhouse gases in the near term, although unlikely, does exist.

After a 1985 report shocked the world with news of the antarctic ozone hole, the offending chemicals were soon targeted under a 1987 international treaty, the Montreal Protocol. The United Nations–sponsored agreement set aggressive phaseout targets for the use of ozone-depleting chemicals in developed countries. This treaty has been very successful. It focuses additional attention on developing countries, which were granted a grace period under the original treaty. Not every country has as yet ratified the protocol and all of its subsequent amendments, but enough have done so to make a serious impact for the better.

According to the United Nations Environment Program, "Developed countries ended the use of CFCs [chlorofluorocarbons] faster and with less cost than was originally anticipated. Scientists predict that ozone depletion will reach its worst point in the next few years and then gradually decline until the ozone layer returns to normal around 2050, assuming the Montreal Protocol is fully implemented."[66]

Survival of the Antarctic Treaty system

While climate and ozone issues command a much bigger global stage, local issues throughout Antarctica will continue to put pressure on the Antarctic Treaty system. The commerce-driven demands for fishing and tourism will require serious attention, as will the minerals issue when the fifty-year moratorium is up for review.

"It gives me no satisfaction to conclude that environmental protection will probably retreat in importance," predicted Bill Bush, a former Australian diplomat, at a 2001 conference. "Environmental interests will undoubtedly be under pressure from a larger commercial presence."[67]

However, the Antarctic Treaty system has survived thus far because of international commitment and cooperation.

Territorial Claims

Although the Antarctic Treaty does not recognize the territorial claims laid by seven countries involved in the region's early exploration, it does not eliminate them either. Any disruption or dissolution of the treaty system could lead some or all of those countries to reassert their prior claims, possibly amid great controversy. International law and Antarctica expert Christopher Joyner suggests that the original claims by Britain, France, Australia, Norway, New Zealand, Argentina, and Chile are not valid because actual occupation and peaceful control over territory is the accepted international requirement for sovereign ownership. Since no native population of people exists, he suggests that actual colonization of a territory would have to take place in order to claim sovereignty.

"Merely sighting some hitherto unknown Antarctic land, going ashore, planting a flag, and proclaiming title in the name of a foreign regent was not enough," Joyner states. Furthermore, he says, "the physical challenges of Antarctica make effective occupation almost impossible to achieve." In other words, simply operating a small research base at one location does not technically qualify as occupation and control over a territory.

However, if environmental conditions are so harsh as to prohibit the fulfilling of accepted international standards, Joyner wonders, "should international law make exceptions . . . for regions deemed to be uninhabitable?" That question remains unanswered, and will for a long time if the Antarctic Treaty continues to work as it did over its first forty years.

Through the foresight of its drafters, the Antarctic Treaty possesses the capacity for change. However, the participating nations have resisted calls for making Antartica a "world park," a request made by various organizations over the last three decades. Since such a term remains practically and legally undefined, the ATS countries prefer the current governing regime. In fact, many say that the strict environmental regulations of the last protocol, along with the ban on mining, make Antarctica as close to a world park as one could get.

"The continent at least still remains essentially pristine," remarked Beth Clark, executive director of the Antarctica Project.

> The big question is whether it's going to stay that way. Nobody's saying that Antarctica should be off-limits to human activities. Not many are arguing that there should be no commercial fishing in the Southern Ocean. Right now, we have a choice: we can continue the way we are going, exploiting resources throughout the world and moving into the Antarctic when nowhere else is left. Or we can decide that one part of the world, at least, is going to be treated differently, left largely alone and allowed to remain the way it has been for millions and millions of years.[68]

Notes

Introduction

1. Quoted in Alastair Fothergill, *A Natural History of the Antarctic.* New York: Sterling, 1995, p. 29.

2. David Walton, "Antarctica's Tainted Horizons," *Unesco Courier*, May 1999, p. 13.

Chapter 1: The Great Frozen Continent

3. Quoted in Roff Smith, "Antarctica, Life at the Bottom of the World," *National Geographic,* December 2001, p. 26.

4. Quoted in Creina Bond and Roy Siegfried, *Antarctica: No Single Country, No Single Sea.* New York: Mayflower Books, 1979, p. 89.

5. Quoted in Bond and Siegfried, *Antarctica: No Single Country, No Single Sea*, p. 100.

6. Quoted in David Helvarg, "Elegant Scavengers," *E Magazine*, November/December 1999, p. 25.

7. Quoted in Mariana Gosnell, "Meltdown: Warm Weather Is Melting Antarctic Ice," *International Wildlife*, July/August 1998, p. 18.

Chapter 2: Human Impact on a Fragile Land

8. Quoted in Helvarg, "Elegant Scavengers," p. 26.

9. Walton, "Antarctica's Tainted Horizons," p. 11.

10. Quoted in *Ross Sea Region 2001: A State of the Environment Report for the Ross Sea Region of Antarctica.* Christchurch, New Zealand: New Zealand Antarctic Institute, 2001, p. 312.

11. Quoted in Ian Snape, Martin J. Riddle, and Jonathan S. Stark, Coleen M. Cole, Catherine K. King, Sabine Duquesne and Damian B. Gore, "Management and remediation of contaminated sites at Casey Station, Antarctica," Australian Antarctic Division, Polar Record 37 (202), 2001, p. 200.

12. Jeff Rubin, *Lonely Planet Antarctica.* Oakland, CA: Lonely Planet, 2000, p. 56.

13. Quoted in "Soils and Permafrost," in part II of *A Framework for Assessing Environmental Impacts of Possible Antarctic Mineral Development.* Columbus, OH: Ohio State University Institute for Polar Studies, 1977, p. E-31.

14. Quoted in D.W.H. Walton, "Life in a Cold Environment," *Antarctic Science.* Cambridge, UK: Cambridge University Press, 1987, p. 137.

15. Quoted in Kieran Mulvaney, "The Last Wild Place," *E Magazine*, November/December 1997, p. 37.

16. Quoted in Robert J. Hofman and Joyce Jatko, "Assessment of the Possible Cumulative Environmental Impacts of Commercial Ship-Based Tourism in the Antarctic Peninsula Area," National Science Foundation, Proceedings of a Workshop Held in La Jolla, CA, June 7–9, 2000, p. 19.

17. Bond and Siegfried, *Antarctica: No Single Country, No Single Sea*, p. 156.

18. Quoted in John May, *The Greenpeace Book of Antarctica: A New View of the Seventh Continent.* London: Doubleday, 1989, p. 132.

19. Quoted in Mulvaney, "The Last Wild Place," p. 38.

20. Quoted in Mulvaney, "The Last Wild Place," p. 40.

21. Quoted in Mulvaney, "The Last Wild Place," p. 40.

22. J. Scott, quoted in Thomas Bauer, *Tourism in the Antarctic.* Binghamton, NY: Howarth Hospitality Press, 2001, p. 136.

23. R.D. Goodman, quoted in Bauer, *Tourism in the Antarctic*, p. 133.

24. Quoted in Hofman and Jatko, "Assessment of the Possible Cumulative, Environmental Impacts of Commercial Ship-Based Tourism in the Antarctic Peninsula Area," p. 13.

25. Quoted in Smith, "Antarctica: Life at the Bottom of the World," pp. 33–34.

26. Quoted in Walton, "Antarctica's Tainted Horizons," p. 11.

Chapter 3: Eye on the Minerals

27. Deborah Shapley, *The Seventh Continent.* Washington, DC: Resources for the Future, 1985, p. 134.

28 Quoted in "Antarctic Marine Geology and Geophysics," in part II of *A Framework for Assessing Environmental Impacts of Possible Antarctic Mineral Development*, 1977, p. B-13.

29. Quoted in Shapley, *The Seventh Continent*, p. 139.

30. Quoted in Shapley, *The Seventh Continent*, pp. 139–140.

31. Quoted in Mulvaney, "The Last Wild Place," p. 39.

32. Quoted in Sharon Levy, "Can Oiled Seabirds Be Rescued or Are We Just Fooling Ourselves?" *National Wildlife*, February/March 1999, p. 70.

33. Quoted in "Marine Biology," in part II of *A Framework for Assessing Environmental Impacts of Possible Antarctic Mineral Development*, p. H-14.

34. Quoted in "Marine Biology," p. H-22.

35. Quoted in "Marine Biology," p. H-14.

36. Quoted in Shapley, *The Seventh Continent*, p. 139.

37. Quoted in "Glaciology and Hydrology," in part II of *A Framework for Assessing Environmental Impacts of Possible Antarctic Mineral Development*, p. C-3.

38. Quoted in part I of *A Framework for Assessing Environmental Impacts of Possible Antarctic Mineral Development*, p. VII-25.

39. Quoted in part I of *A Framework for Assessing Environmental Impacts of Possible Antarctic Mineral Development*, p. VII-25.

40. Quoted in "Avian Populations," in part II of *A Framework for Assessing Environmental Impacts of Possible Antarctic Mineral Development*, p. J-13.

41. Quoted in "Meteorological Considerations," in part II of *A Framework for Assessing Environmental Impacts of Possible Antarctic Mineral Development*, pp. F29–30.

42. Shapley, *The Seventh Continent*, p. 127.

43. Quoted in part I of *A Framework for Assessing Environmental Impacts of Possible Antarctic Mineral Development*, p. XI-3.

44. Quoted in Walter Sullivan, *Frozen Future, A Prophetic Report from Antarctica.* New York: Quadrangle Books, 1973, p. 44.

Chapter 4: A Changing Climate

45. Quoted in *British Antarctic Survey,* "Climate Change Causes Extreme Changes to Antarctic Lakes," January 21, 2002. www.antarctica.ac.uk.

46. Quoted in Smith, "Antarctica: Life at the Bottom of the World," pp. 27–31.

47. Quoted in Smith, "Antarctica: Life at the Bottom of the World," p. 27.

48. Quoted in Carol Kaesuk Yoon, "Penguins in Trouble Worldwide," *New York Times*, June 26, 2001. www.nytimes.com.

49. Quoted in *National Science Foundation,* "Giant Icebergs, Unprecedented Ice Conditions Threaten Antarctic Penguin Colonies," December 26, 2001. www.nsf.gov.

50. Quoted in Kevin Krajick, "Tracking Icebergs for Clues to Climate Change," *Science*, June 22, 2001, p. 2245.

51. Quoted in Robert Barr, "Antarctic Ice Shelf Collapses," Associated Press, March 19, 2002.

52. Quoted in Barr, "Antarctic Ice Shelf Collapses."

53. Quoted in Sid Perkins, "Antarctic Sediments Muddy Climate Debate," *Science News*, September 8, 2001, p. 150.

54. Quoted in *Stanford University,* "Antarctic Mud Reveals Ancient Evidence of Global Climate Change," December 19, 2001. www.stanford.edu.

55. Quoted in *Stanford University,* "Antarctic Mud Reveals Ancient Evidence of Global Climate Change."

56. Quoted in *New York Times*, "Melting of Antarctic Ice Sheet Is Linked to Ancient History," October 12, 1999.

57. Quoted in Malcolm W. Browne, "Under Antarctica, Clues to an Icecap's Fate," *New York Times*, October 26, 1999.

58. Quoted in *New York Times*, "Fish Damage Linked to UV," March 18, 1997.

59. Quoted in *Ross Sea Region*, p. 5.42.

Chapter 5: Vigilance for Antarctica

60. Christopher C. Joyner, *Governing the Frozen Commons:* The Antarctic Regime and Environmental Protection. Columbia: University of South Carolina Press, 1998, p. 21.

61. Robert Rutford, Testimony before the Committee of Science, *United States House of Representatives,* April 18, 1996. www.house.gov.

62. Quoted in *Antarctican*, "Russia on Brink of Antarctic Shutdown," Sept. 5, 2001. www.antarctican.com.

63. Bauer, *Tourism in the Antarctic*, p. 4.

64. Quoted in *Antarctican*, "Polar Tourism's Big Shake-Up," July 16, 2001. www.antarctican.com.

65. Quoted in *Antarctican*, "Polar Tax Fight Cooling," January 20, 2002. www.antarctican.com.

66. "Basic Facts and Data on the Science and Politics of Ozone Depletion," United Nations Environment Program, October 5, 2001, p. 6.

67. Quoted in *Antarctican*, "Warning of Future Antarctic Discord," June 26, 2001. www.antarctican.com.

68. Quoted in Mulvaney, "The Last Wild Place," p. 41.

Glossary

ablation: All processes that remove material from a glacier, including melting, evaporation, or calving.

chlorofluorocarbon (CFC): A chemical compound of fluorine, carbon, and chlorine that is broken down into its components by the stronger sunlight (UV) at high altitudes and causes damage to the ozone.

calving: The action by which icebergs form by breaking off an ice shelf or glacier and falling into the ocean or a lake.

fast ice: The more stable part of sea ice that is close to shore.

hydrocarbon: One of a very large group of chemical compounds composed only of carbon and hydrogen; the largest source of hydrocarbons is petroleum crude oil.

hypothermia: A potentially fatal condition of abnormally low body temperature, brought on by exposure to extreme cold.

ice shelf: A large flat-topped sheet of ice that is attached to land along one side and floats in an ocean or lake. More ice is added to the ice shelf from flow of the ice on land and from new snow. Ice is removed from the ice shelf by calving and melting.

metabolite: A substance produced by, or necessary for, metabolism, the chemical processes necessary for processing nutrients within an organism.

ozone: A naturally occurring gas in the stratosphere that creates a protective barrier for the Earth's surface by blocking much of the potentially damaging ultraviolet radiation that comes from the sun.

pack ice: The more unstable part of sea ice that floats well away from shore, often in large pieces.

permafrost: Permanently frozen subsoil, occurring through-out the polar regions and in perennially frigid areas.

rookery: A breeding ground or colony of some birds and mammals.

stratosphere: An upper portion of the Earth's atmosphere, beginning several miles above the Earth's surface. Ozone forms naturally here.

UV-B radiation: A harmful form of ultraviolet radiation that is usually filtered out by the atmosphere's ozone layer in the stratosphere.

Organizations
to Contact

Antarctic and Southern Ocean Coalition/
The Antarctica Project
1630 Connecticut Ave. NW
3rd Floor
Washington, DC 20009
(202) 234-2480
e-mail: antarctica@icg.org
www.asoc.org

The Antarctica Project is the only conservation organization in the world that works exclusively for Antarctica. This nongovernmental, nonprofit organization leads the international Antarctic and Southern Ocean Coalition (ASOC), made up of 240 member groups in fifty countries, to ensure that the environment comes first when decisions are made under the Antarctic Treaty system.

Antarctica New Zealand
Private Bag 4745
Christchurch
New Zealand
e-mail: info@antarcticanz.govt.nz
www.antarcticanz.govt.nz

Antarctica New Zealand is responsible for developing, managing, and administering New Zealand activities in Antarctica and the Southern Ocean, particularly in the Ross Sea.

Antarctic Wildlife Research Unit
School of Zoology
University of Tasmania
GPO Box 252-05, Hobart
Tasmania 7001, Australia
+61 3 6226 2645
e-mail: Mark.Hindell@utas.edu.au
www.zoo.utas.edu.au/awru/AWRU1020.htm

The Antarctic Wildlife Research Unit (AWRU) at the University of Tasmania is an ecological research group run at the School of Zoology.

Australian Antarctic Division
Channel Highway
Kingston, Tasmania 7050
Australia
+61 3 6232 3209
e-mail: information@aad.gov.au
www.aad.gov.au

The Australian Antarctic Division (AAD), a part of the Australian government's Department of the Environment and Heritage, has the responsibility of administering Australia's wide-ranging activities in antarctic and subantarctic regions.

British Antarctic Survey
High Cross, Madingly Road
Cambridge CB3 0ET
United Kingdom
+44(0) 1223 221400
e-mail: information@bas.ac.uk or schools@bas.ac.uk
www.antarctica.ac.uk

The British Antarctic Survey (BAS), an institute of the Natural Environment Research Council, has undertaken most of Britain's research on and around the continent of Antarctica.

Byrd Polar Research Center
The Ohio State University
1090 Carmack Road, Scott Hall, Room 108

Columbus, OH 43210-1002
(614) 292-6531
e-mail: lyons.142@osu.edu
www-bprc.mps.ohio-state.edu

The Byrd Polar Research Center is recognized internationally as a leader in polar and alpine research, with programs conducted throughout the world. Studies focus on the role of cold regions in the global climate system, with major research on climatic reconstruction of glacial and postglacial times; polar ice sheets: high-latitude landform evolution, soils, and hydrology; geologic evolution of Antarctica; and the history of polar exploration.

Commission for the Conservation of Antarctic Marine Living Resources

P.O. Box 213
North Hobart 7002
Tasmania, Australia
e-mail: ccamlr@ccamlr.org
www.ccamlr.org

The Convention on the Conservation of Antarctic Marine Living Resources came into force in 1982, as part of the Antarctic Treaty system, in response to concerns that an increase in krill catches in the Southern Ocean could have a serious effect on populations of krill and other marine life; particularly on birds, seals, and fish, which depend mainly on krill for food.

Council of Managers of National Antarctic Programs

Suite 25, Salamanca Square, Hobart, Tasmania 7000
GPO Box 824, Hobart, Tasmania 7001
Australia
+61 3 6233 5498
e-mail: jsayers@comnap.aq
www.comnap.aq

The Council of Managers of National Antarctic Programs (COMNAP) brings together those managers of national agencies responsible for the conduct of Antarctic operations in the support of science.

Environmental Defense Fund
257 Park Avenue South
New York, NY 10010
(212) 505-2100
e-mail: press@environmentaldefense.org
www.environmentaldefense.org

The Environmental Defense Fund is a leading national non-profit organization linking science, economics, and law to create innovative, equitable, and cost-effective solutions to society's most urgent environmental problems.

Greenpeace
702 H Street NW, Suite 300
Washington, DC 20001
(202) 462-1177
e-mail: greenpeace.usa@wdc.greenpeace.org
www.greenpeace.org

Greenpeace is a nonprofit organization with a presence in forty countries across Europe, the Americas, Asia, and the Pacific. It does not accept donations from governments or corporations, but relies on contributions from individual supporters and foundation grants, and focuses on the most crucial worldwide threats to the planet's biodiversity and environment.

Institute of Antarctic & Southern Ocean Studies
University of Tasmania
GPO Box 252-77, Hobart
Tasmania 7001, Australia
+61 (03) 6226 2971
e-mail: Kelvin.Michael@utas.edu.au
www.antcrc.utas.edu.au

The Institute of Antarctic and Southern Ocean Studies (IASOS) is a postgraduate teaching and research center established at the University of Tasmania to promote and focus Australian academic activity concerned with Antarctica and its surrounding ocean.

International Association of Antarctica Tour Operators
P.O. Box 2178
Basalt, CO 81621
(970) 704-1047
e-mail: iaato@iaato.org
www.iaato.org

A member organization founded to advocate, promote, and practice safe and environmentally responsible private-sector travel to the Antarctic.

National Geographic Society
1145 17th Street NW
Washington, DC 20036-4688
(800) 647-5463
e-mail: askngs@nationalgeographic.com
www.nationalgeographic.com

The National Geographic Society is the world's largest non-profit scientific and educational organization.

National Snow and Ice Data Center
449 UCB
University of Colorado
Boulder, CO 80309-0449
(303) 492-6199
e-mail: nsidc@nsidc.org
www.nsidc.org

Part of the National Oceanic and Atmospheric Administration, serving as a national information and referral center in support of polar and cryospheric research. Maintains information about snow cover, avalanches, glaciers, ice sheets, freshwater ice, sea ice, ground ice, permafrost, atmospheric ice, paleoglaciology, and ice cores.

National Wildlife Federation
1400 16th Street NW
Washington, DC 20036-2266
(800) 822-9919
www.nwf.org

The National Wildlife Federation is the nation's largest member-supported conservation group, uniting individuals, organizations, businesses, and government to protect wildlife, wild places, and the environment.

Natural Resources Defense Council
40 West 20th Street
New York, NY 10011
(212) 727-2700
e-mail: nrdcinfo@nrdc.org
www.nrdc.org

The Natural Resources Defense Council uses law, science, and the support of its 500,000 members to protect the planet's wildlife and wild places and to ensure a safe and healthy environment for all living things.

Scientific Committee on Antarctic Research
Scott Polar Research Institute
Lensfield Road
Cambridge CB2 1ER
United Kingdom
+44 1223 362061 or 336550
e-mail: execsec@scar.demon.co.uk
www.scar.org

The Scientific Committee on Antarctic Research (SCAR) is a committee of the International Council for Science, and it is charged with the initiation, promotion, and coordination of scientific research in Antarctica. SCAR also provides international, independent scientific advice to the Antarctic Treaty system.

Scott Polar Research Institute
Lensfield Road
Cambridge CB2 1ER
United Kingdom
+44 (0) 1223 336540
e-mail: enquiries@spri.cam.ac.uk
www.spri.cam.ac.uk

The Institute at the University of Cambridge is a well-known center for research into both polar regions.

Seal Conservation Society
7 Millin Bay Road
Tara, Portaferry
County Down BT22 1QD
Ireland
+44-(0)28-4272-8600
e-mail: info@pinnipeds.org
www.pinnipeds.org

A nonprofit, charitable organization, the society strives to protect and conserve seals worldwide.

Smithsonian Institution
P.O. Box 37012
SI Building, Room 153, MRC 010
Washington, DC 20013-7012
(202) 357-4300
e-mail: info@si.edu
www.si.edu

The Smithsonian Institution is the world's largest museum complex and research organization, composed of sixteen museums and galleries, as well as the National Zoo.

United Nations Environment Program
North American Region
1707 H Street, #300
Washington, DC 23006
(202) 785-0465
e-mail: info@rona.unep.org
www.unep.org

This program seeks to provide leadership and encourage partnership in caring for the environment by inspiring, informing, and enabling nations and peoples to improve their quality of life without compromising that of the future generations. This includes the protection of wildlife, habitats, and the Earth's atmosphere.

U.S. Antarctic Marine Living Resources
Southwest Fisheries Science Center
8604 La Jolla Shores Drive

La Jolla, CA 92037-1508
(858) 546-7000
e-mail: swfsc.web@noaa.gov
swfsc.ucsd.edu/Antarctic.htm

This section of the National Oceanic and Atmospheric Administration is responsible for the U.S. Antarctic Marine Living Resources (AMLR) Program, a basis for U.S. policy on the management and conservation of antarctic living resources. The program supports U.S. participation in the Commission for the Conservation of Antarctic Living Marine Resources.

U.S. National Science Foundation Office of Polar Programs

National Science Foundation
4201 Wilson Boulevard
Room 755
Arlington, VA 22230
(703) 292-8030
e-mail: dmarsha@nsf.gov
www.nsf.gov

This department of the National Science Foundation fosters research on global and regional problems of current scientific importance, to utilize the region as a platform or base from which to support research. The U.S. Antarctic Program (USAP) supports only that research that can be done exclusively in Antarctica or that can be done best from Antarctica.

World Wildlife Fund

1250 24th Street NW
Washington, DC 20037
(202) 293-4800
www.worldwildlife.org

The World Wildlife Fund is dedicated to protecting the world's wildlife and wildlands, directing its conservation efforts toward three global goals: protecting endangered spaces, saving endangered species, and addressing global threats.

For Further Reading

Books

Antarctica: The Extraordinary History of Man's Conquest of the Frozen Continent. Surry Hills, NSW, Australia: Reader's Digest, 1990. Good overview of Antarctic history and environment.

Alastair Fothergill, *A Natural History of the Antarctic: Life in the Freezer.* New York: Sterling, 1995. Award-winning book about Antarctica's natural life, with extensive photography accompanying text.

Periodicals

Kieran Mulvaney, "The Last Wild Place," *E Magazine*, November/December 1997. Reviews the various environmental challenges facing Antarctica at the turn of the century.

Roff Smith, "Antarctica, Life at the Bottom of the World," *National Geographic*, December 2001. Traces some of the current scientific and tourist activity in various areas of the Antarctic.

Websites

Cool Antarctica (www.coolantarctica.com). Contains a wealth of educational information and photographs about Antarctica, as well as links to other Antarctica sites. This site is run by a marine biologist and teacher who spent two years there with the British Antarctic Survey.

McMurdo Station virtual tour (astro.uchicago.edu).
Provides a photographic virtual tour of the McMurdo station
and other Antarctica subjects, with accompanying text
and links.

Nature: The World of Penguins (www.pbs.org). Website
companion to this PBS program about penguins.

Works Consulted

Books

Thomas Bauer, *Tourism in the Antarctic.* Binghamton, NY: Howarth Hospitality Press, 2001. Detailed information on the challenges and opportunities facing tourism operators in Antarctica.

Jim Bishop, Launcelot Fleming, Paul Goodall-Copestake, Jonathan Walton, and Kevin Walton, *Portrait of Antarctica.* London: George Philip, 1984. A photo-dominated look at Antarctica's natural world, with some accompanying text.

Creina Bond and Roy Siegfried, *Antarctica: No Single Country, No Single Sea.* New York: Mayflower Books, 1979. A "mosaic" of Antarctica and the Southern Ocean in words and pictures, revealing the natural world there, with an eye toward the political realities and challenges of conservation.

A Framework for Assessing Environmental Impacts of Possible Antarctic Mineral Development. Parts I and II. Columbus, OH: Ohio State University Institute for Polar Studies, 1977. An exhaustive academic study commissioned by the United States government for analyzing a variety of environmental and wildlife issues relating to mineral development in Antarctica.

Philip Jessup and Howard Taubenfeld, *Controls for Outer Space, and the Antarctic Analogy.* New York: Columbia University Press, 1959. Analyzes the antarctic political situation just prior to the Antarctic Treaty's signing and applies it to parallel issues regarding the use and control of outer space.

Christopher C. Joyner, *Governing the Frozen Commons: The Antarctic Regime and Environmental Protection.* Columbia: University of South Carolina Press, 1998. Academic study of the Antarctic Treaty system and how it operates, as well as what legal innovations may be necessary in the future to address political and economic development issues.

John May, *The Greenpeace Book of Antarctica: A New View of the Seventh Continent.* London: Doubleday, 1989. Good overview of antarctic history and environment, along with the organization's proposals for conservation.

Ron Naveen, Colin Monteath, Tui De Roy, and Mark Jones, *Wild Ice: Antarctic Journeys.* Washington, DC: Smithsonian Institution Press, 1990. Collection of essays by four writers/ photographers on the beauty and challenges of Antarctica.

Ross Sea Region 2001: A State of the Environment Report for the Ross Sea Region of Antarctica. Christchurch, New Zealand: New Zealand Antarctic Institute, November 2001. A thorough and current assessment of wildlife, environment, and human presence in the Ross Sea area of Antarctica, as well as conservation efforts in the region.

Jeff Rubin, *Lonely Planet Antarctica.* Oakland, CA: Lonely Planet, 2000. Technically a travelers' guide to Antarctica, but also a comprehensive overview of the history, environment, and the various political issues.

Deborah Shapley, *The Seventh Continent.* Washington, DC: Resources for the Future, 1985. Explores the antarctic ecosystem while analyzing the many environmental and wildlife issues faced under the Antarctic Treaty system.

Walter Sullivan, *Frozen Future: A Prophetic Report from Antarctica.* New York: Quadrangle Books, 1973. An American perspective on science and politics of Antarctica published ten years after the Antarctica Treaty's signing.

D.W.H. Walton, *Antarctic Science.* Cambridge, UK: Cambridge University Press, 1987. A review of all of the scientific disciplines and subjects being utilized in antarctic research, with attention to the Antarctic Treaty system.

Periodicals/Reports

Robert Barr, "Antarctic Ice Shelf Collapses," Associated Press, March 19, 2002.

Mary Batten, "Alerting the World to Save Antarctica," *The Calypso Log*, February 1990.

BioScience, "Ecological Legacies: Impacts on Ecosystems of the McMurdo Dry Valleys," December 1999.

David H. Bromwich and Thomas R. Parish, "Antarctica: Barometer of Climate Change," Report to the National Science Foundation, Antarctic Meteorology Workshop, June 1998.

Malcolm W. Browne, "Oil and Fishing Force Penguins to Hunt Afar as Chicks Starve," *New York Times*, June 10, 1997.

————, "Under Antarctica, Clues to an Icecap's Fate," *New York Times*, October 26, 1999.

————, "Russians Scale Back Research at South Pole," *New York Times*, August 13, 1999.

————, "Ice Shifts May Be Tied to Warming," *New York Times*, November 18, 1997.

————, "South Pole Gets Colder," *New York Times*, August 26, 1997.

Steve Chapman, "Environmental Pessimism Confronts Reality," *Chicago Tribune*, October 28, 2001.

Amanda Cooper, "Mining World Seeks Natural Remedy for Toxic Waste," *Reuters News Service*, October 23, 2001.

Cornelia Dean, "In an Antarctic Desert, Signs of Life," *New York Times*, February 3, 1998.

Erik Eckholm, "129 Nations Agree on Funds for Ozone Shield," *New York Times*, December 4, 1999.

Elizabeth Finkel, "Major Changes Proposed in Antarctica," *Science*, November 14, 1997.

Fort Worth Star-Telegram, "Ice Sheet Thickening, Not Melting, Scientists Say," January 18, 2002.

Henry Fountain, "Discovering Early Clues to Where an Albatross Wanders on Its Year Off," *New York Times*, September 5, 2000.

———, "Two Gigantic Icebergs Break Free from the Antarctic Ice Cap," *New York Times*, April 11, 2000.

Sarah T. Gille, "Warming of the Southern Ocean Since the 1950s," *Science*, February 15, 2002.

Mariana Gosnell, "Meltdown: Warm Weather Is Melting Antarctic Ice," *International Wildlife*, July/August 1998.

Thomas Hayden and Sharon Begley, "Cold Comfort," *Newsweek*, August 11, 1997.

Martin Hayes, "Mining Cleans Up, Embraces Cutting Edge Technology," *Reuters News Service*, October 23, 2001.

David Helvarg, "Elegant Scavengers," *E Magazine*, November/December 1999.

———, "Antarctica: The Ice Is Moving," *E Magazine*, September 2000.

Alan Hemmings, "Antarctica in Transition," *Forest & Bird*, 1997.

Bryan Hodgson, "Alaska's Big Spill: Can the Wilderness Heal?" *National Geographic*, January 1990.

Robert J. Hofman and Joyce Jatko, "Assessment of the Possible Cumulative Environmental Impacts of Commercial Ship-Based Tourism in the Antarctic Peninsula Area," National Science Foundation, Proceedings of a Workshop Held in La Jolla, CA, June 7–9, 2000.

Jocelyn Kaiser, "Is Warming Trend Harming Penguins?" *Science*, June 20, 1997.

Richard Kerr, "Climate Change: A Single Climate Mover for Antarctica," *Science*, May 3, 2002.

Kevin Krajick, "Tracking Icebergs for Clues to Climate Change," *Science*, June 22, 2001.

Sharon Levy, "Can Oiled Seabirds Be Rescued or Are We Just Fooling Ourselves?" *National Wildlife*, February/March 1999.

Edwin McDowell, "Antarctica Isn't Orlando, but Crowds Are a Worry," *New York Times*, February 14, 1999.

John G. Mitchell, "In the Wake of the Spill: 10 Years After the *Exxon Valdez*," *National Geographic*, March 1999.

Richard Monastersky, "The Strangest Home on Earth: Looking for Frosty Life in a Lake Under Antarctica," *Science News*, October 2, 1999.

New York Times, "Fish Damage Linked to UV," March 18, 1997.

———, "Antarctica May Carry Clues to Climate Trends," August 23, 1998.

———, "Melting of Antarctic Ice Sheet Is Linked to Ancient History," October 12, 1999.

Sid Perkins, "Antarctic Sediments Muddy Climate Debate," *Science News*, September 8, 2001.

Andrew C. Revkin, "Antarctic Test Raises Hope on a Global-Warming Gas," *New York Times*, October 12, 2000.

———, "Record Ozone Hole Refuels Debate on Climate," *New York Times*, October 10, 2000.

Mark Sincell, "Supernova Clues Found in Antarctic Ice," *Astronomy*, January 2000.

Raymond C. Smith, "Exploring Sea Ice Indexes for Polar Ecosystem Studies," *BioScience*, February 1998.

Ian Snape, Martin J. Riddle, Jonathan S. Stark, Coleen M. Cole, Catherine K. King, Sabine Duquesne, and Damian B.

Gore, "Management and remediation of contaminated sites at Casey Station, Antarctica," Australian Antarctic Division, Polar Record 37 (202), 2001.

David W. J. Thompson and Susan Solomon, "Interpretation of Recent Southern Hemisphere Climate Change," *Science*, May 3, 2002.

USA Today, "Lakes Under Antarctic Ice Could Hide Life," June 18, 2001.

Warwick F. Vincent, "Icy Life on a Hidden Lake," *Science*, December 10, 1999.

David Walton, "Antarctica's Tainted Horizons," *Unesco Courier*, May 1999.

Paul Webster, "Russia Can Save Kyoto, If It Can Do the Math," *Science*, June 21, 2002.

Alexandra Witze, "Lake Study Underscores Climate Shift-Ecology Link," *Dallas Morning News*, January 28, 2002.

———, "Krill Found to Swarm Under Antarctic Sea Ice," *Dallas Morning News*, March 11, 2002.

Jack Williams, "Pole Microbes Survive a Hard Life," *USA Today*, July 7, 2000.

Carol Kaesuk Yoon, "Penguins in Trouble Worldwide," *New York Times*, June 26, 2001.

———, "Antarctica's Frigid Waters Form Evolutionary Cauldron," *New York Times*, March 9, 1999.

Internet Sources

Antarctican, "Warning of Future Antarctic Discord," June 26, 2001. www.antarctican.com.

———, "Polar Tourism's Big Shake-Up," July 16, 2001. www.antarctican.com.

———, "Russia on Brink of Antarctic Shutdown," September 5, 2001. www.antarctican.com.

————, "Polar Tax Fight Cooling," January 20, 2002. www.antarctican.com.

British Antarctic Survey, "Climate Change Causes Extreme Changes to Antarctic Lakes," January 21, 2002. www. antarctica.ac.uk.

National Science Foundation, "Giant Icebergs, Unprecedented Ice Conditions Threaten Antarctic Penguin Colonies," December 26, 2001. www.nsf.gov.

Robert Rutford, Testimony before the Committee of Science, *U.S. House of Representatives,* April 18, 1996. www.house.gov.

Stanford University, "Antarctic Mud Reveals Ancient Evidence of Global Climate Change," December 19, 2001. www.stanford.edu.

Websites

Alfred Wegener Institute for Polar and Marine Research (Germany) (www.awi-bremerhaven.de). Conducts research in antarctic, arctic, and temperate latitudes. Research, reports, and resource information available.

Amundsen–Scott South Pole Station virtual tour (www.astro.uchicago.edu). Provides a photographic virtual tour of the U.S. South Pole station and other Antartica subjects, with accompanying text and links.

Antarctic Experience (www.gdargaud.net). Site maintained by French researcher in Antarctica, featuring a variety of information and photography.

Antarctic Treaty (webhost.nvi.net). Searchable database for reviewing the Antarctic Treaty and subsequent legislation.

Antarctica Earth Science (www.glacier.rice.edu). This website, run by the West Antarctic Ice Sheet Study, seeks to introduce antarctic Earth science to students. Research, reports, and resource information available, with other data and links.

The Antarctican (News) (www.antarctican.com). This website seeks to deliver the latest news and comment on "Antarctic life, South Polar endeavors, the world of the ice, and the Southern Ocean around it."

Canadian Polar Commission (www.polarcom.gc.ca). Contains information on the research, reports, and resources of this group and the Canadian Committee on Antarctic Research.

Environmental Action (www.environmentalaction.net). Site provides conservation information and links in a call to action to protect the Earth's wildlife and habitats.

French Polar Institute (www.ifremer.fr). Contains information on the research, reports, and resource information of this group.

Heritage Antarctica (www.heritage-antarctica.org). The website of a coalition of national Antarctic Heritage Trusts, which have joined to promote the restoration, preservation, and protection of the structures, artifacts, and records that reflect the history of human endeavor in Antarctica.

Japan's National Institute of Polar Research (www.nipr.ac.jp). Contains information on the research, reports, and resource information of this group.

New South Polar Times (205.174.118.254/nspt/home/htm). On-line newsletter written by the staff of the Amundsen–Scott South Pole station, South Pole, Antarctica.

Norwegian Polar Institute (www.npolar.no). Contains information on the research, reports, and resource information of this group.

Penguin Page (www.users.capu.net). Thorough resource on all species of penguins and their natural world.

70South (www.70south.com). Contains a wealth of news, educational information, and photographs about Antarctica, as well as links to other Antarctica sites. This site is run by a Belgian researcher who has worked in Antarctica.

South African National Antarctic Program (www. sanap.org). Contains information on the research, reports, and resource information of this group.

South Pole Observatory (www.cmdl.noaa.gov). The Climate Monitoring and Diagnostics Laboratory (CMDL) of the National Oceanic and Atmospheric Administration conducts sustained observations and research related to trends and global distributions of atmospheric constituents that are capable of forcing change in the climate of the Earth.

United Nations Framework Convention on Climate Change (www.unfccc.int). Contains background and current information on the research, reports, and resource information of this group, dedicated to stabilizing the Earth's atmosphere and climate by limiting man-made greenhouse gases worldwide.

University of Cambridge Center for Atmospheric Science/Ozone Hole (www.atm.ch.cam.ac.uk). Thorough examination of the ozone hole problem over Antarctica.

Index

Picture Credits

Cover Image: © Peter Johnson/CORBIS
© Associated Press, AP, 88
© Tim Davis/Photo Researchers, 22
© Natalie Fobes/CORBIS, 55
© Robert W. Hernandez/Photo Researchers, 10
© George Holton/Photo Researchers, 37
© Hulton Archive, 52
© Hulton-Deutsch Collection/CORBIS, 64
© Peter Johnson/CORBIS, 57
Chris Jouan, 15, 69
© Joyce Photographs/Photo Researchers, 34
© National Oceanic & Atmospheric Association, 13, 14, 17,
   20, 24, 41, 73, 78
© Newsmakers/Getty Images, 72
PhotoDisc, 7, 8, 19, 27, 63
© Chris Rainier/CORBIS, 84
© Galen Rowell/CORBIS, 76, 81, 82
© Joy Russell/Reuters/Getty Images, 42, 44
© Telegram, Keith Gosse, 59
© Michael Van Woert, NOAA NEDSIS, ORA, 49
© Wisconsin-Madison/Reuters/Getty Images, 67

About the Author

Dennis Roberson is a freelance writer living in Fort Worth, Texas. While growing up he developed an avid interest in science, history, travel, and the outdoors. He has journeyed extensively to wilderness areas and national parks, backpacking primarily throughout western North America. He attended the University of Texas, where he received his degree in journalism. He has written an award-winning regional interest book that was honored by the San Antonio Conservation Society for helping to preserve Texas culture and traditions. When not writing, Roberson manages a professional golf tournament in Fort Worth.